knots

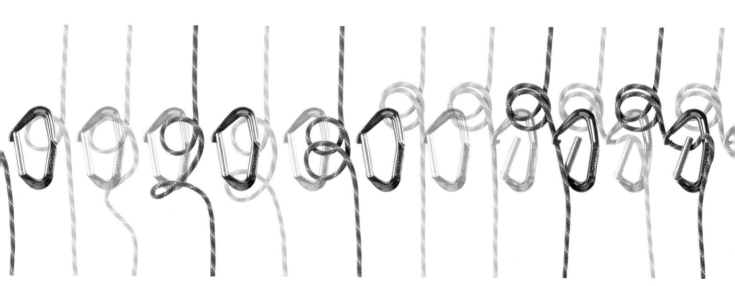

a *flow*motion™ title

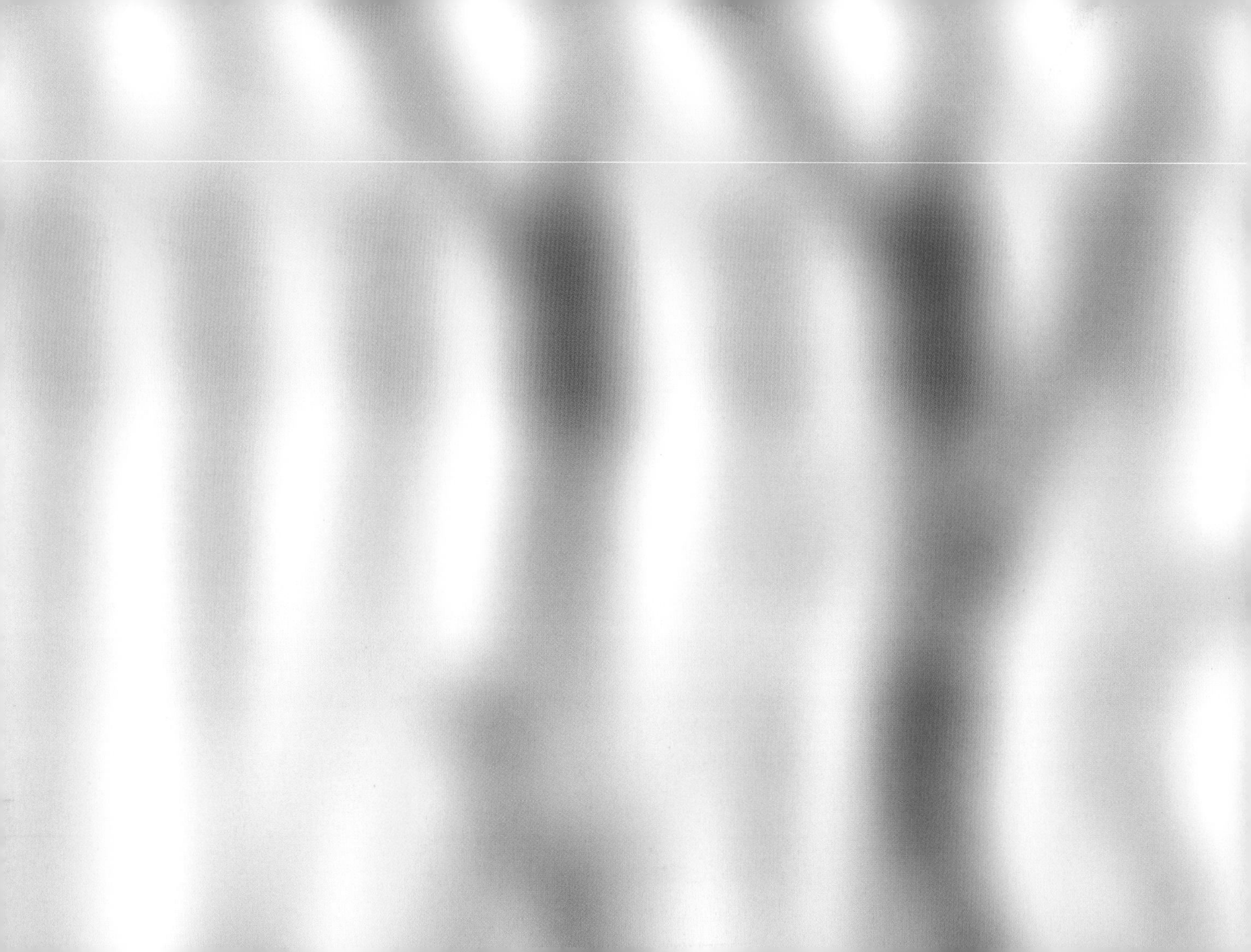

knots

geoffrey budworth

Sterling Publishing Co., Inc.
New York

Created and conceived by
Axis Publishing Limited
8c Accommodation Road
London NW11 8ED
www.axispublishing.co.uk

Creative Director: Siân Keogh
Managing Editor: Brian Burns
Project Designer: Sean Keogh
Project Editor: Antony Atha
Production Manager: Sue Bayliss
Production Controller: Juliet Brown
Photographer: Mike Good

Library of Congress Cataloging-in-Publication
Data Available

10 9 8 7 6 5 4 3 2 1

Published in 2003 by Sterling Publishing Co., Inc.
387 Park Avenue South, New York, NY 10016
Text and images © Axis Publishing Limited 2003
Distributed in Canada by Sterling Publishing
c/o Canadian Manda Group,
One Atlantic Avenue, Suite 105
Toronto, Ontario, Canada, M6K 3E7

ISBN 0–8069–9377–4

Printed by Star Standard (Pte) Limited

a *flowmotion*™ title

knots

contents

introduction

Nobody should be at a loss when it comes to tying a load on to a car rack, tying a first-aid tourniquet, or rigging up a child's swing. Tying knots is a fundamental skill, and, similar to the ability to read a map, swim, change a fuse, or wire a plug, it brings a sense of reassuring self-reliance. Knotting can also be a fascinating and pleasant pastime—as absorbing as puzzle solving, but with far greater practical applications.

history
Knotting know-how emerged in the Stone Age, long before mankind learned to harness wind or wave power, cultivate the soil, or use fire. According to historians, knots predate the invention of the wheel by thousands of years. Our ancestors used knots for many crucial tasks: going underground in search of ores and fuel, hauling up water from deep wells, catching fish, making shelters, and securing loads to pack animals who ventured with their owners across unmapped territories in search of trade and treasure. Knots were also used to keep a count of trading transactions and to remember tribal lore. Weapons of war, such as the longbow and siege engines like the rock-throwing mangonel, also relied upon knotted cordage for their effectiveness.

Knots have since been used by individuals as diverse as: balloonists and bookbinders; cobblers and cowboys; farmers and firefighters; gardeners and poachers; prospectors and sailors; shopkeepers and surgeons; and truckers and weavers.

Today, the International Guild of Knot Tyers, a registered US educational charity, caters for the worldwide resurgence of interest in the study and practice of knotting as an art, craft, and science.

knotting terms and terminology

The collective name for the long, thin, round, and flexible material in which knots are tied is cordage. Anything with a diameter of more than $^1/_3$in (10mm) is called a rope, although any rope with a particular use is commonly referred to as a line (for example, a mooring line, washing line, and towing line). Cordage smaller than a rope is known as cord (if it is braided) or string (if it is twisted). Good quality stuff of the thinnest diameters is customarily sold as thread, twine, or cotton.

Knots that join (or bend) two ropes together are referred to as bends. Those that attach a line to a rail, ring, spar, or post are called hitches. The exception to this rule is when a ring or eyelet is involved, in which case the knot may be called a bend, as sailors speak of bending a line to a ring or eye. For example, the anchor bend illustrated on pages 54–55 is, in fact, a hitch.

Only something that is neither a bend nor a hitch is, strictly speaking, a knot. Knots include stoppers, bindings, shortenings, and loops. Anything tied in string, twine, or other thin stuff (as all cordage is commonly called), for example fishing line, is simply a knot. This explains why the fisherman's knot (pages 28–29), the double fisherman's knot (pages 30–31), and the blood knot (pages 32–33) are located in the section dealing with bends.

The active end of any line involved in tying a knot is called the working, free, or running end. The other, often inert, end is called the standing end, and the section in between is the standing part.

When an end or standing part is bent into a U-shape, this is referred to as a bight. When a bight acquires a crossing point, it becomes a loop. If the part nearest the working end goes beneath, it is an underhand loop, as opposed to when it goes on top and forms an overhand loop. A couple

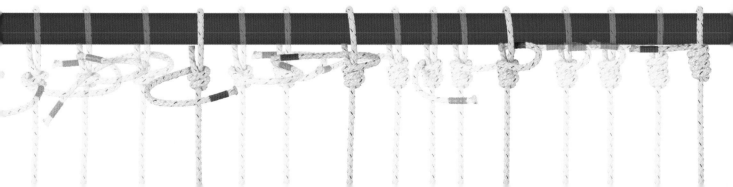

of crossing points close together, one over, the other under, creates interlocked elbows. Knotted loops may be fixed or sliding. A sliding loop is commonly known as a noose.

When the working end is not pulled completely through a completed knot but is left protruding in the form of a bight, this is known as a drawloop, and many of the knots featured in this book can be tied with one. The drawloop is a quick-release device and such a knot is therefore called a slipped knot.

strength and security

The strength of a knot is a measure of how well it preserves the breaking strength of the type of cordage in which it is tied. A simple overhand knot can reduce it by more than half, so that knot is said to be (at best) 50 percent efficient. Many hitches, such as the ossel knot (pages 46–47), have a strength in excess of 80 percent, and a few knots may even be rated close to 100 percent. In other words, they are almost as strong as the unknotted rope or cord.

Knot security is an entirely different quality. If a knot slips, capsizes, and falls apart for any reason, then it is less secure than one that doesn't in similar conditions. The bowline (pages 66–67) is a fairly strong knot, but can come undone if tied in a stiff or slippery line such as bungee cord or shock elastic, so it is a less secure knot than the perfection loop (pages 70–71), which, although it may not be much stronger, holds firm in bungee cord and is very secure.

A bight with a crossing point forms a loop. When the working end goes underneath, it is an underhand loop, as shown here; on top it forms an overhand loop.

WORKING END

Two crossing points close together, one over and one under, make interlocking elbows.

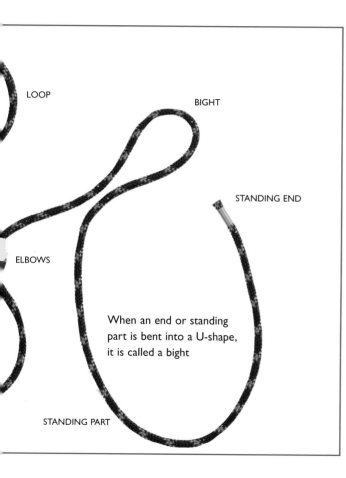

LOOP

BIGHT

STANDING END

ELBOWS

When an end or standing part is bent into a U-shape, it is called a bight

STANDING PART

The strength and security of any knot depends ultimately upon how and where the friction operates. This is known as the nip, and can be either concentrated (as in sheet bends and bowlines) or distributed (as in the figure-of-eight bend and the slide-and-cling hitch).

materials and construction

Ropes were once all made from fibers obtained from natural matter, such as flax and jute plant stems; sisal and abaca (hemp) leaves; the fibrous coating attached to the outside of cotton seeds and coconut shells (coir); horse and camel hair; esparto grass, reeds, and date palms; and wool and silk. The fibers were shredded, teased, combed, and graded, then twisted (right-handed) into yarns. A number of yarns were then counter-twisted (left-handed) to form strands, which were finally twisted and closed up (right-handed once more) to make the rope. These twists and counter-twists gave rope its strength and durable handling qualities. Ropes still made with three strands in this traditional style are called hawsers and are said to be hawser-laid.

Today, most cordage materials are made from synthetic materials. The most common are the four "Ps"—polyamide (trade name Nylon), polyester (trade names Terylene and Dacron), polypropylene, and polyethylene (Polythene). There are also the so-called "super" fibers, such as Kevlar and Spectra, or HMPE (also marketed as Dyneema).

Synthetic fiber ropes can also be hawser-laid, but, more commonly, they consist of a braided outer covering that encloses a large number of core filaments. The core itself can be hawser-laid or plaited, or can consist of parallel yarns. These ropes are called sheath-and-core (kernmantel, in the case of climbing ropes of European origin) or braid-on-braid, depending upon the actual construction.

Ropes of sheath-and-core and braid-on-braid construction are stronger and generally more flexible than hawser-laid ones. They have other desirable properties too. For instance, nylon ropes are exceptionally elastic, capable of stretching under a load and resuming their true length again when the load is removed. This preserves more of their breaking strength by yielding to absorb at least some of the energy of a sudden load, making them the natural choice for ropes used in climbing or caving and for boat anchor warps and towing lines.

Terylene is very strong and does not stretch as much as nylon. This makes it ideal for rigging masts and aerials, or for any other role where stretch is unwanted.

Many hi-tech ropes combine desirable qualities so that it is possible to have a nylon line (for elasticity) sheathed in terylene (to withstand abrasion); or a terylene rope (for strength) with a fluffy matt polypropylene outer covering (for comfortable handling).

TYPES OF ROPE CONSTRUCTION

The 3-strand rope is the oldest and simplest form of rope construction. Three-strand ropes are still made and are called hawsers. The majority of modern ropes are made from synthetic materials and can be multiplait, 6-strand, 12-strand, braidline, or superline. Each one is constructed in a different way depending on the purpose for which it is intended.

8 PLAIT DYNEEMA CORE
16 PLAIT POLYESTER COVER

3 STRAND POLYESTER CORE
16 PLAIT POLYESTER COVER

3 STRAND POLYESTER CORE
16 PLAIT POLYESTER COVER

PARALLEL LAID POLYPROPYLENE CORE
16 PLAIT POLYPROPYLENE COVER

3 STRAND POLYESTER COVER
16 PLAIT POLYESTER COVER

3 STRAND POLYESTER COVER
16 PLAIT POLYESTER COVER

8 PLAIT DYNEEMA CORE
8 PLAIT POLYPROPYLENE INTERMEDIATE CORE
16 PLAIT POLYESTER COVER

LOOKING AFTER CORDAGE

Cheap and cheerful string can be cut off and discarded after use. More costly cordage can be cared for in the following ways:

- Whip, tape, or heat-seal cut ends to prevent them unravelling.
- Coil rope and hang it up so that it is not trodden underfoot.
- Prevent prolonged exposure to the UV radiation of sunlight.
- Avoid exposure to acid, alkalis, and other chemicals.
- Do not subject synthetics to heat—direct, indirect, or through friction—that could glaze or even melt them.
- Dry vegetable fiber cordage that has become wet before storage.
- Hose ropes down to remove abrasive dirt, grit, or salt water.
- Wash ropes in water with a mild detergent at least once a year.
- Combat wear and tear by changing a rope's position periodically to vary the points of wear in use, or swap the rope end for end. Alternatively, wrap vulnerable spots with plastic or rubber tubing.
- Inspect cordage periodically for danger signs, such as broken outer fibers, visibly damaged inner fibers (hawser-laid ropes only), a ruptured sheath, or one that has crept over its core and formed wrinkles.
- Keep a diary of usage for life-support ropes, discarding or downgrading them to less vital work when their history indicates excessive wear.

learning to tie knots

Avoid hard-laid ropes that have been tightly tensioned during manufacture, as they will be stiff and awkward to handle. Soft-laid, flexible cordage is preferable. All the knots in this book can be learned by practicing on two lengths of soft-laid, flexible cordage, each of which should be no more than ¼in (6mm) in diameter and about a yard (or meter) in length. Long braided boot laces, round in cross-section, are a neat alternative. When tying bends, it may help if the two cords are different colors.

Yacht ropes, climbing ropes, and accessory cords are expensive because they are made to the highest specifications; they are subjected to the greatest strains and human lives depend on their reliability. Unless you plan to use rope for these purposes, buy cheaper alternatives. Camping and caravan outlets, as well as hardware and dry goods stores, stock a variety of polypropylene ropes and cords at more affordable prices.

asher's principle of do-and-undo

Knots may be more easily learned from a person, but most of us manage well enough with the next best thing—a knot book. There is a Catch 22 element to learning how to tie any knot from the printed page, as the tying steps will only make sense if you know what the completed knot looks like, yet you must first tie it in order to see the final outcome. The Flowmotion presentation allows you to scan the knotting process

backward, as well as forward, so you can gain a good idea of what you are doing and where you are going. Sports coaches and other teachers of practical skills call this the "whole-part-whole" method and use it a lot.

The tying method chosen and illustrated for each knot in this book is one that can be clearly portrayed and described. With practice, many of the knots can be tied more speedily, at least one other way. Discover how by undoing any knot (a tuck at a time) and pausing to see how it is constructed. Then reassemble it. Often, in retying, an obvious shortcut will occur to you. Do it that way next time. This do-&-undo process of self-instruction was first described by the knotting writer and researcher Dr. Harry Asher in 1989.

TYING TIPS

■ Use the simplest knot for the job in hand, but do not sacrifice knot strength and security just for the sake of simplicity.

■ Tie every knot correctly. One mistaken tuck or turn can turn a reliable knot into a killer. Distorting a knot when tightening it can have the same effect.

■ Arrange each knot with care, then tighten it. Knots with extra twists or poorly tightened knots are weaker and less reliable.

■ If what is to be bound is soft and yielding (the neck of a sack, for example), tie binding knots in hard-laid cordage so the knot will bite effectively. An exception is bandages on living creatures.

■ If what is to be seized is hard (for example, a metal rail), tie binding knots in soft-laid cordage as the knot grips best this way.

■ Do NOT use binding knots, such as the reef and constrictor knots, as bends or hitches. They are not designed for those roles.

■ Learn to tie knots with your eyes closed, in the dark, one-handed, behind your back, and in other awkward positions.

■ Keep a length of cord handy and practice tying knots in spare moments.

■ A knot, once learned, should last a lifetime. If you forget knots between using them and needing to use them again, you never really learned them in the first place.

■ Teach knots to others, not only to infect them too with an itch to tie knots, but also as a means of enhancing your own understanding.

asher's law of loop, hitch, and bight

Slide any hitch off its foundation to see what happens. If it falls apart and vanishes, then that hitch could have been tied "in the bight," that is, without using either end. This is a great way to discover improved tying methods, and all knot tyers should work out alternative methods of tying knots that suit them. Try the constrictor knot (pages 114–115) and the strangle knot (pages 120–121). The former collapses, so it can be tied in the bight. The latter ends up as an overhand knot, so it cannot be tied in the bight. As a general rule, tying in the bight is not only quicker and easier, but enables you to impress onlookers with your speed and dexterity.

Similarly, if a loop can be untied by simply removing a bight, then that knot too may be tied in the bight. Examples of this are the perfection loop (pages 70–71), the alpine butterfly (pages 72–73), and the scaffold knot (pages 80–81). This previously unrecognized relationship was another discovery by Dr. Harry Asher.

go with the flow

The special Flowmotion images used in this book have been created to show the whole process of tying each knot, using different colored cordage to enable this to be easily understood. Each knot sequence is shown across the page from left to right, demonstrating how the knot progresses. Consult the finished knot to check that you have tied it correctly. Each knot is carefully explained with step-by-step captions.

Below this, another layer of information in the timeline breaks the knot into its various parts. These will help you to tie the knot correctly. Knot-making is something that everyone does the whole of their lives, and not enough people give tying knots enough thought. Knots are designed for a specific purpose. Knowing how to tie the right knot at the right time avoids accidents and might even help you to save a life.

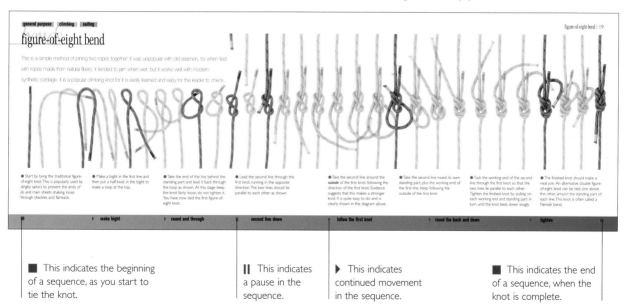

general purpose   climbing   sailing

figure-of-eight bend

figure-of-eight bend | 19

This is a simple method of joining two ropes together. It was unpopular with old seamen, for when tied with ropes made from natural fibers, it tended to jam when wet, but it works well with modern synthetic cordage. It is a popular climbing knot for it is easily learned and easy for the leader to check.

● Start by tying the traditional figure-of-eight knot. This is popularly used by dinghy sailors to prevent the ends of jib and main sheets shaking loose through shackles and fairleads.

● Make a bight in the first line and then put a half-twist in the bight to make a loop at the top.

● Take the end of the line behind the standing part and lead it back through the loop as shown. At this stage keep the knot fairly loose; do not tighten it. You have now tied the first figure-of-eight knot.

● Lead the second line through the first knot, running in the opposite direction. The two lines should lie parallel to each other as shown.

● Take the second line around the **outside** of the first knot, following the direction of the first line. Evidence suggests that this makes a stronger knot. It is quite easy to do and is clearly shown in the diagram above.

● Take the second line round its own standing part, plus the working end of the first line. Keep following the outside of the first knot.

● Tuck the working end of the second line through the first knot so that the two lines lie parallel to each other. Tighten the finished knot by pulling on each working end and standing part in turn until the knot beds down snugly.

● The finished knot should make a neat join. An alternative double figure-of-eight knot can be tied, one above the other, around the standing part of each line. This knot is often called a Flemish bend.

■   ▶ make bight   ▶ round and through   ‖ second line down   ▶ follow the first knot   ▶ round the back and down   ▶ tighten   ■

■ This indicates the beginning of a sequence, as you start to tie the knot.

‖ This indicates a pause in the sequence.

▶ This indicates continued movement in the sequence.

■ This indicates the end of a sequence, when the knot is complete.

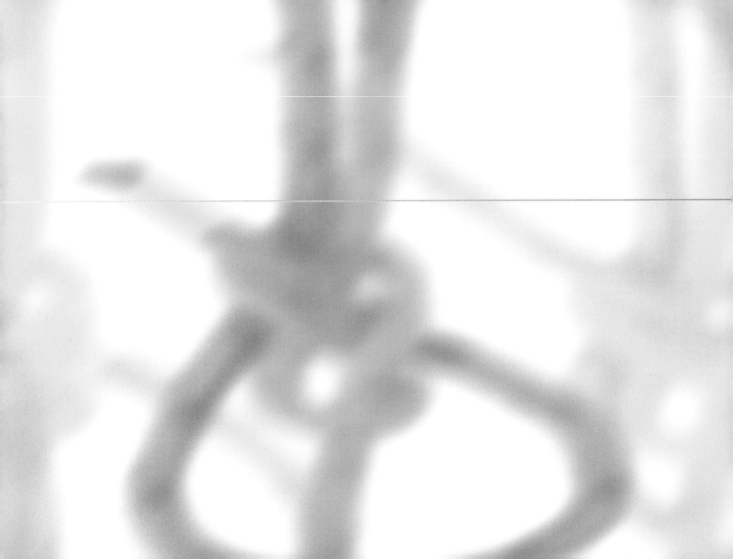

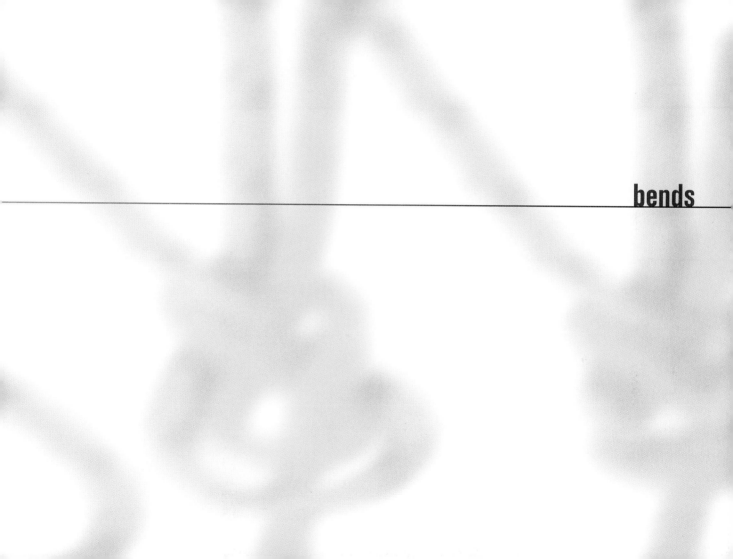

bends

figure-of-eight bend

This is a simple method of joining two ropes together. It was unpopular with old seamen, for when tied with ropes made from natural fibers, it tended to jam when wet, but it works well with modern synthetic cordage. It is a popular climbing knot for it is easily learned and easy for the leader to check.

● Start by tying the traditional figure-of-eight knot. This is popularly used by dinghy sailors to prevent the ends of jib and main sheets shaking loose through shackles and fairleads.

● Make a bight in the first line and then put a half-twist in the bight to make a loop at the top.

● Take the end of the line behind the standing part and lead it back through the loop as shown. At this stage keep the knot fairly loose; do not tighten it. You have now tied the first figure-of-eight knot.

● Lead the second line through the first knot, running in the opposite direction. The two lines should lie parallel to each other as shown.

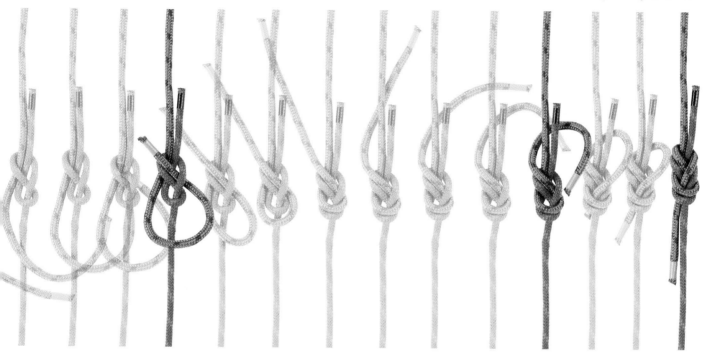

● Take the second line around the *outside* of the first knot, following the direction of the first knot. Evidence suggests that this makes a stronger knot. It is quite easy to do and is clearly shown in the diagram above.

● Take the second line around its own standing part, plus the working end of the first line. Keep following the outside of the first knot.

● Tuck the working end of the second line through the first knot so that the two lines lie parallel to each other. Tighten the finished knot by pulling on each working end and standing part in turn until the knot beds down snugly.

● The finished knot should make a neat join. An alternative double figure-of-eight knot can be tied, one above the other, around the standing part of each line. This knot is often called a Flemish bend.

▶ **follow the first knot**　　　　　　　　▶ **around the back and down**　　　　　▶ **tighten**

zeppelin bend

This knot is both strong and secure and was traditionally used by the U.S. Navy to secure lighter-than-air ships—hence its name. It can be tied using any weight of line.

● The basis of the Zeppelin bend is the simple overhand knot, a knot frequently used by sailors to stop ropes unreeving from shackles, or as the basis of the angler's and turle knots used by fishermen.

● It is simplicity itself. Make a loop with your line or rope and bring the end back to the front of the standing part of the rope.

● Pass the end of the rope through the loop from right to left. Make sure to leave the knot loose at this stage so that you can run the second rope through easily.

● If you are using this knot to join two lengths of rope, you need only allow for a short length of the second rope to pass through the first knot.

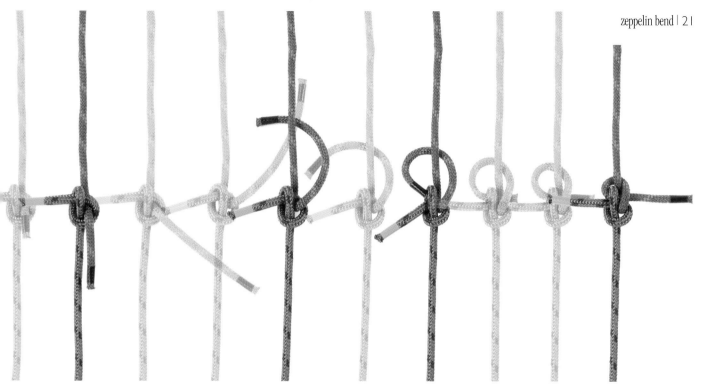

● Bring the second rope, illustrated in red, down through the loop formed in the first knot. This rope goes through the loop from back to front as shown in the picture above. Make sure you do this correctly.

● When you have taken enough rope through the loop, take the end of the rope up and around the back of the standing part of the rope.

● Bring the rope down; then pass it through both loops from left to right. The first loop is the top of the first knot; the second is the loop made by the overhand knot of the second rope.

● Tighten both knots to finish. This makes a neat knot, with the end of the first rope leading away to the left and the end of the second rope leading away to the right The knot is both strong and secure.

adjustable bend

This is a climber's bend where the two knots are left apart. Subjected to steady strain, they remain apart, but under a sudden extra load the knots will slide together and absorb some of the shock.

● Lay the two lengths of line parallel to each other. Then wrap one of the lines around the other, wrapping it toward the working end.

● Take two complete turns around the line. The adjustable bend has a good deal in common with the rolling hitch, a traditional naval knot used to absorb a lateral pull.

● After the second turn, take the working end around and under both lines and then bring it back down in front of the second line, tucking it under its own final turn. Do not tighten the knot completely.

● Tie the same knot with the second line around the first. You can work from the opposite end as shown here or turn the lines end for end.

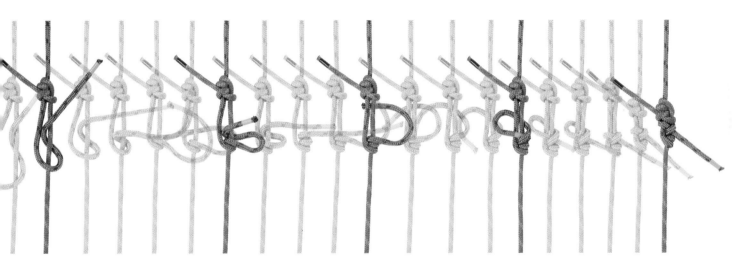

● Make two complete turns as before. When tying the second knot, you have to pass the working end of the line through the bight formed by the first knot.

● Complete the second knot by taking the working end behind both lines and then back down in front of the first line, trapping the working end under its own final turn.

● Tighten both knots but leave them apart. The knots may have from 6in (5cm) to a yard (meter) of space between them.

● Under sudden strain the knots will slide together as shown. This helps the rope to absorb any sudden impact, such as when a climber falls. The bend was invented by the Canadian climber Robert Chisnall.

▶ **repeat with the second rope**   ▶ **tighten both knots**

bends one-way sheet bend

The sheet bend is one of the first knots that all sailors learn and is generally used either to make a temporary join in two ropes or as a temporary mooring hitch. It is not particularly strong or secure. The one-way sheet bend is a refinement on the basic knot and is designed to make the bend streamlined so that the ropes can be pulled through obstructions or towed through the water more easily.

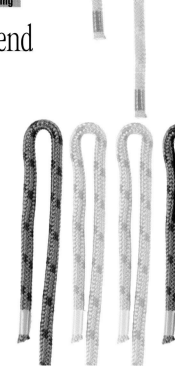

● Make a bight in the first line. The sheet bend is normally used to join lines of similar thickness; the double sheet bend is used for lines of different thickness.

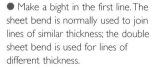

● Lead the working end of the second line through the bight and then take it around the back of both parts of the first line.

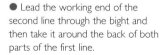

● Tuck the end of the second line underneath itself so that both the short ends are on the same side of the knot. This completes the standard sheet bend that can be tightened at this point.

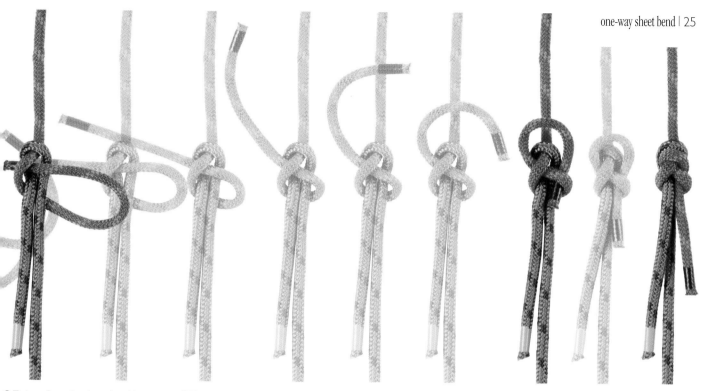

● To transform the sheet bend into a one-way sheet bend, take the working end of the second line around and back on itself. This makes a figure-of-eight knot.

● Tuck the working end down to complete the figure-of-eight, bringing it down at the front. It does not go behind the standing part of the second line.

● Tuck the end in and pull the knot tight. The two short ends and the standing part of the first line are now all pointing in the same direction.

● Make sure that the three ends all point away from the direction in which the knot is being pulled. The knot is now less likely to snag on any obstacle.

through in front   **around and down**

surgeon's knot

This popular knot forms a neat bend and can be tied with all sizes of rope. It can be used for wrapping parcels and is more secure than the ordinary reef knot on which it is based. It is not used at sea, for it can jam when tied with ropes made from natural fibers. It was probably used by military surgeons for sutures and would have been tied using catgut.

● Take the two ropes to be joined and lay them side by side. Cross the working ends of the two ropes.

● When tying the surgeon's knot or reef knot, it is easiest to cross the ropes in sequence with the left hand rope crossing over the right to start with. Make a simple half knot as you would when tying a bow.

● Take an additional turn with one of the working ends. It does not matter which one you use. This is what gives the knot its additional strength.

make a single overhand knot

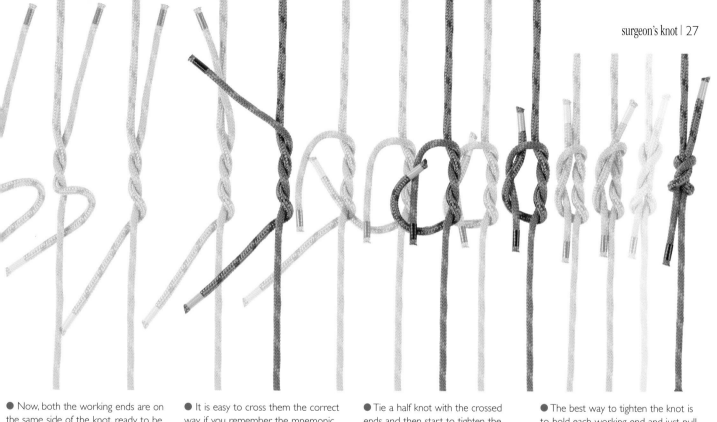

● Now, both the working ends are on the same side of the knot, ready to be crossed in the opposite direction to the first stage of the knot.

● It is easy to cross them the correct way if you remember the mnemonic "left over right, right over left." Another way to cross them correctly is to lay the working end of the rope on the same side as the standing part.

● Tie a half knot with the crossed ends and then start to tighten the knot. As can be seen, without the extra turn, this would be a simple reef knot.

● The best way to tighten the knot is to hold each working end and just pull on the standing part. This makes the upper part of the knot twist slightly so that it lies over the completed knot from corner to corner.

▶ **take a second turn**   ▶ **make an overhand knot**   ▶ **tighten**

fisherman's knot

This is a useful and extremely simple knot that can be used for a wide variety of purposes. It is perfectly secure tied with rope or string. It originated as a knot used by 18th and 19th century anglers for joining two lengths of horse hair or catgut. However, with the advent of fine nylon leaders, the single fisherman's knot, shown here, fell from favor as it was prone to slip.

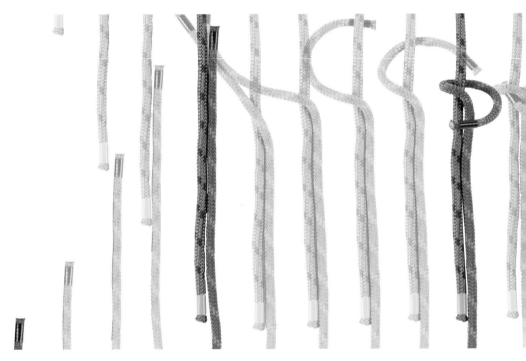

● Lay two lengths of rope or twine alongside each other.

● Take the working end of one rope and tie a simple overhand knot around the standing part of the second rope.

● Take the first rope around the second and make the knot so that the working end points up toward the standing part of the second rope. Pull the knot until it is firm but do not overtighten it.

● Take the working part of the second rope and tie a similar overhand knot around the standing part of the first rope. Make sure that you allow sufficient rope to give you a fairly long free end.

● When both knots have been completed, the two ropes will lie parallel to each other, with the free ends of the ropes pointing in opposite directions.

● Tighten the knots by pulling on their respective working ends, but leave enough play in them so that they can slide toward each other.

● Pull on the standing parts of each rope to bring the knots tightly together. This unites the knot. When this knot is tied with rope, it can be undone; but if it is tied with string, it will have to be cut apart.

double fisherman's knot

The double fisherman's knot—or the grinner knot—is stronger than the ordinary fisherman's knot, but it is seldom used by fishermen today. The triple fisherman's knot, or double grinner, is a strong knot for joining lengths of nylon, but it is more difficult to tie than the traditional blood knot (see pages 32–33). The double fisherman's knot is reasonably secure under all normal conditions.

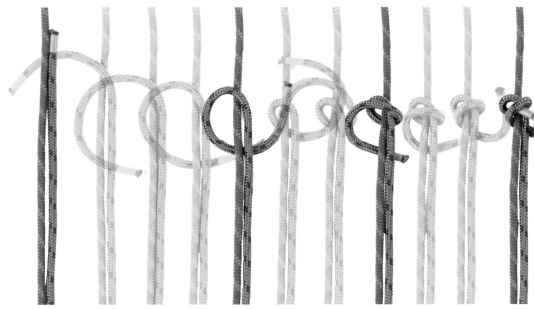

● The principle behind this knot is exactly the same as the single fisherman's knot. Start by laying two lengths of line parallel with each other.

● Make a loop with the first line around the standing part of the second line, and then overlay a second turn on top of the first turn.

● The working end of the first line is then taken down below the two turns and tucked under them both. Pull the first knot secure but not too tight.

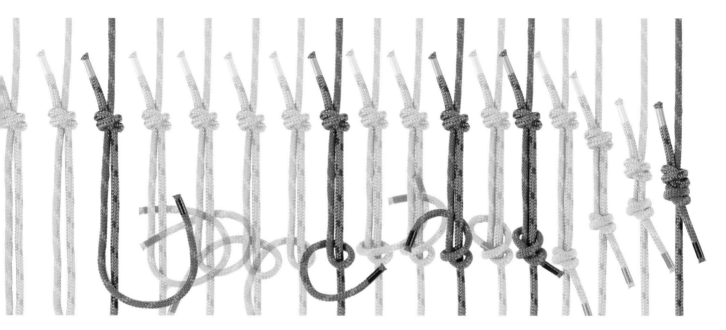

● Once the first knot has been completed, make an identical second knot with the second line around the standing part of the first line. Pull enough rope through so that you can tie the knot easily.

● Make the first turn around the first line and then lay another turn on top. The picture sequence shows the progression of the knot clearly.

● After the second turn has been completed, trap the working end under both turns so that it points down the first line. Pull the knot tight.

● When the knots are tight, pull on the standing part of both lines to bring the knots together. This knot is easily tied with thick line and makes a secure bend but is much trickier to manage with fine monofilament.

▶ **two turns as before**   ▶ **through and tighten**

blood knot

The blood knot is one of the best ways of joining two lines and forms a secure neat knot. Knots of this type are often called barrel knots. Here the knot is tied with an inward coil, which is easier to do with thicker cordage.

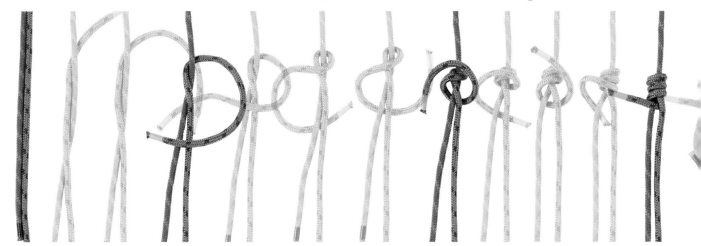

● Lay the two lengths of line to be joined beside each other. Blood knots can only be tied when the diameter of the two lines is roughly similar and are commonly used to produce tapered leaders by anglers.

● Take the first turn around the standing part of the second line. Make sure that this turns goes around both lines so that it traps its own standing part. The knot will not hold unless this happens.

● Wrap the first line at least twice more around the standing part of the second line. Here, three turns have been made. With fine nylon you may need to take four or five to ensure that the knot holds.

● See that the turns are neatly bedded together, and then tuck or trap the working end between the two lines as shown.

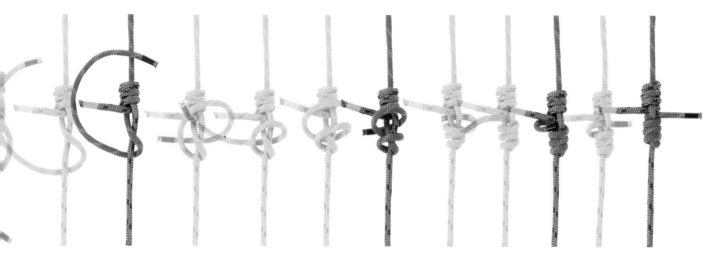

● Repeat the process with the second line. Make sure that the turns are made in the same direction.

● Bed down the first turn carefully to ensure that the standing part of the second line is trapped against the first line. Take the same number of turns with the second line as you did with the first.

● In this case three turns have been taken with each line. Finish the knot by trapping the working end between both lines as shown. The working ends appear on opposite sides of the knot.

● Tighten the working ends first, and then pull on the standing parts to pull the knot neatly together. When tied with fine nylon, it is important to moisten blood knots before tightening.

wrap the second line ▶ **through the opposite way** ▶ **tighten**

carrick bend

The Carrick bend and its near relative the heraldic device, formerly known as the Wake knot—the badge of the Anglo-Saxon leader Hereward the Wake—are two of the oldest knots known. The Carrick bend was traditionally used to join large cables together, a purpose for which its simplicity is ideal. Although it reduces the strength of a cable considerably, it remains a useful knot for this purpose.

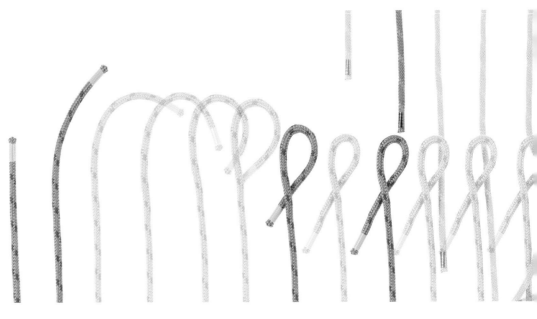

● The heraldic version of the Carrick bend, the Wake knot, has both working ends emerging at the foot of the knot. The device can be found in Elizabethan plasterwork on decorated ceilings.

● The bend tied with the ends emerging at opposite corners is supposedly more secure (as illustrated here). Start by making a loop with the first line, placing the working end under its standing part.

● Bring the second line down under the loop, and then take it across over the standing part of the first line.

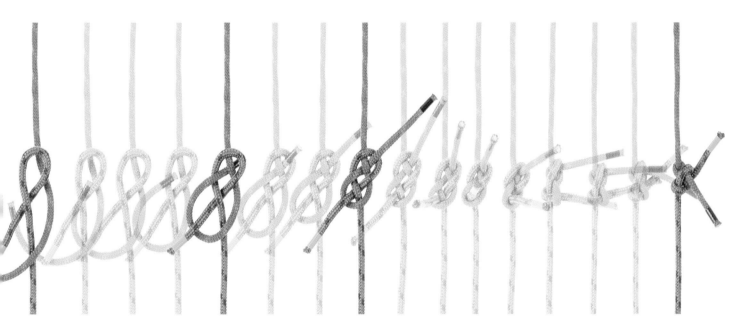

● The second line then goes over the working end of the first line and is led around to the loop. Complete the knot by passing the working end of the second line over the loop, and then under its standing part.

● Finally, trap the lines by taking the line back over the loop. This is easy to tie if you remember the over-under-over sequence. The untightened knot forms an attractive, open device.

● To tie the Wake knot, follow the same steps but working from the opposite direction. The second line goes first under the working part of the first line, and then over the standing part. Both ends emerge adjacent.

● If you are using this knot on land or sea, tighten it by pulling on the standing parts. The knot then collapses into a different shape, as shown above.

▶ **under, over, under, over**　　　▶ **when tightened, the knot capsizes**

simple simon

This is a modern knot that was devised by Harry Asher in 1989, and is one of a series of similar knots. This is the best version when joining cordage of different diameters. It is an excellent knot to secure slippery synthetic lines, for instance while camping in wet weather, and is easily learned.

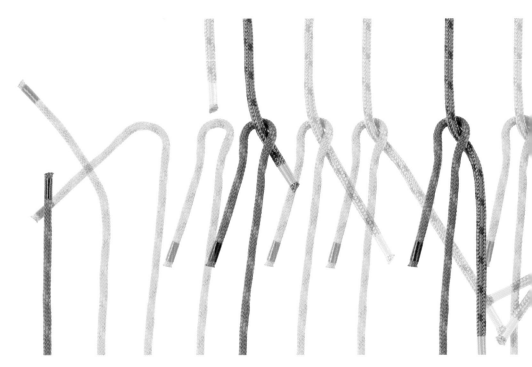

● The original knot is a variation of an unsecured sheet bend, but all the versions start in the same way.

● Make a bight in one of the two lines. Then, bring the working end of the second line over the bight and out to the side, as if you were tying a clove hitch.

● Take a complete turn around both parts of the bight. If you are joining lines of different thickness, always make the knot with the thinner of the two lines, and the loop with the thicker one.

bring the second line through a bight

● Complete the first turn and then wrap a second turn around both parts of the bight.

● When you have laid down the turns neatly, take the working end back through the bight so that the working end lies next to, and parallel with, its own standing part. This is exactly the same principle as the sheet bend.

● Tighten the knot by pulling on the working end and standing part of the second line.

● The knot is now secure. The second turn is pulled across the first, which traps the lines together. All the simple simon knots are easy to learn and tie and are extremely useful in a number of situations.

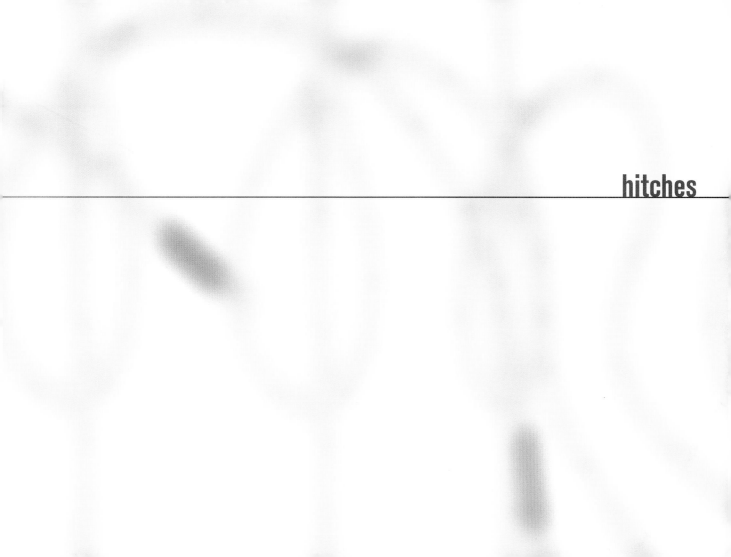

hitches

clove hitch

One of the simplest knots, the clove hitch, can be tied with a working end or in the bight. It is not totally secure and can also jam, so it is best used as a temporary hitch or mooring knot when sailing—usually tied in the bight when the two loops can be dropped over a mooring post or bollard.

● If the clove hitch is tied in the bight (not illustrated), you need to make two loops at a convenient point in the line. Start with an overhand loop, followed by an underhand loop. Make both loops the same size.

● Place the underhand loop on top of the overhand loop, twisting it slightly. The lines should be on the inside of the two loops. Slip the loops over a rail or stanchion and pull on both ends to tighten the hitch.

● Exactly the same knot is shown above, this time tied with a working end. Take the line over the rail (or wherever you want to secure the knot), working from front to back.

● Bring the end up and across the standing part of the line. This can be done in either direction. Here it is shown working from right to left.

▶ take a turn

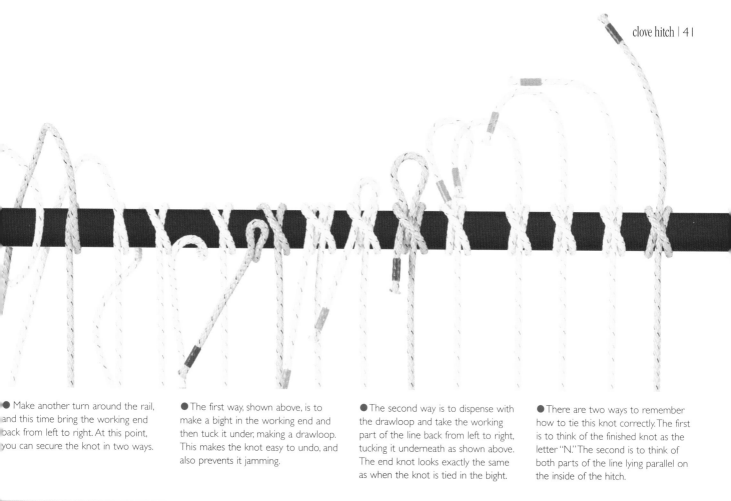

● Make another turn around the rail, and this time bring the working end back from left to right. At this point, you can secure the knot in two ways.

● The first way, shown above, is to make a bight in the working end and then tuck it under, making a drawloop. This makes the knot easy to undo, and also prevents it jamming.

● The second way is to dispense with the drawloop and take the working part of the line back from left to right, tucking it underneath as shown above. The end knot looks exactly the same as when the knot is tied in the bight.

● There are two ways to remember how to tie this knot correctly. The first is to think of the finished knot as the letter "N." The second is to think of both parts of the line lying parallel on the inside of the hitch.

highwayman's hitch

This is one of the knots that might be used in stables for securing horses while they are groomed. It can also be used as a temporary mooring knot for small boats. It is a great trick knot that children love. It looks complicated, but with just a single tug on the short end, it melts away to nothing.

● Although the knot looks complicated, it is actually a series of three loops (bights) all tucked into each other one after the other.

● Make a bight in one end of your rope, and push it behind the hitching rail. You will need to hold it in position with one hand or allow a large enough bight so that it remains in position hanging over the rail.

● Allow a good long working end, as the last stage of the hitch is tied with this. Take up the standing part of the rope and make a second bight the same size as the first, this time in front of the rail.

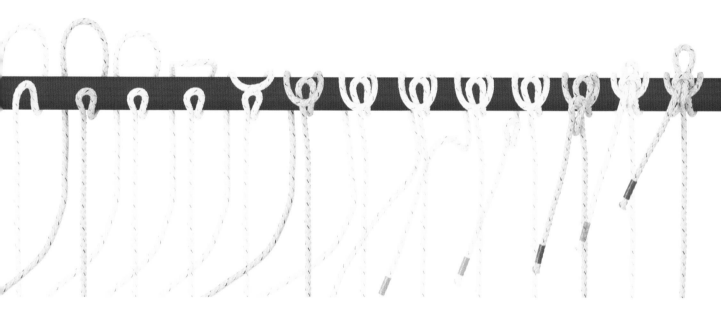

● Pass the second bight through the first as shown. It is easiest if you think of working from the front to the back. This applies to the third stage of the hitch as well as the second.

● When the second bight is through the first, you can secure it by pulling down on the working end. This will free up your hands and make tying the rest of the hitch easier.

● Make a third bight in the working end of your rope, and pass this through the second bight, again from front to back. This time, pull down on the standing part of your rope to make the knot secure.

● The finished hitch shown above looks impregnable and is secure against any pull on the standing part of the rope. However, a sharp tug on the working end will see the hitch melt off the rail as if by magic.

▶ **take the second bight through**   ▶ **make a third bight**   **tighten**

ossel hitch

An "ossel" is a Scottish word
meaning gill net, and this
simple hitch was the knot
used to secure these nets to
the ossel lines that supported
the nets in the sea. The hitch
appears very similar to the
clove hitch, but it is more
secure and cannot be tied "in
the bight." As with so many of
the best knots associated with
the sea, it is very easy to tie.

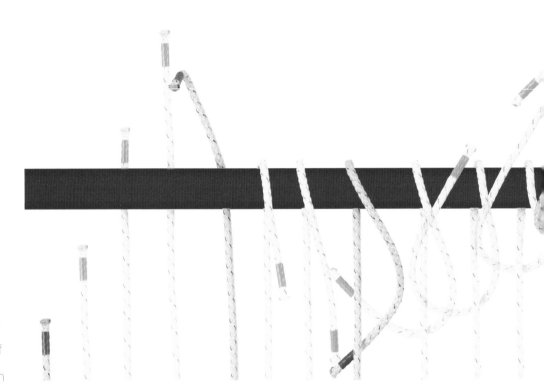

● The ossel hitch can be used
whenever you want a simple, secure
knot that is required to take a steady
strain. It is not designed to withstand
any sustained lateral pull.

● Take a turn behind a post or
another rope and bring the working
end of your line from back to front.
Take the working end around and
behind its standing part as shown.

● The hitch can be tied either way—
from right to left or left to right. Here,
the rope passes from right to left.

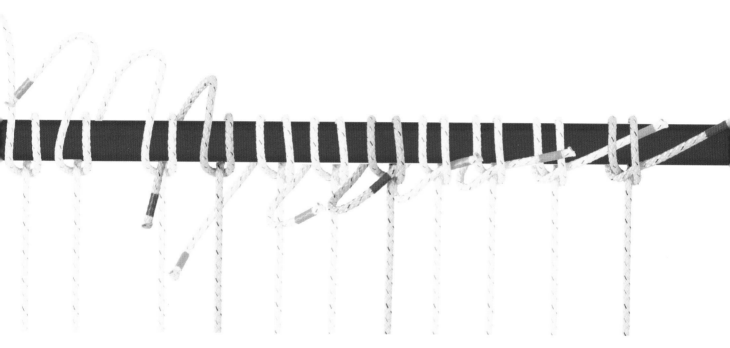

● Make another complete turn around the rail but this time from front to back, not back to front. This forms a bight in the rope with the standing part in the middle.

● Complete the turn and secure the hitch by passing the working end over the turn you have just made and then underneath the first turn.

● Any tension or pull on the standing part now jams the hitch tighter and makes the knot more secure.

● The completed hitch is shown above. This is a typical example of a hitch that can be tied under all circumstances and in all weathers. Apprentice fishermen would learn to tie it with their eyes shut.

▶ **back over**　　　▶ **over and under**　　　▶ **tighten**

ossel knot

The ossel knot is a more secure version of the ossel hitch shown on pages 44–45. This knot was used to secure the drift nets to the upper rope; the hitch was used for the lower.

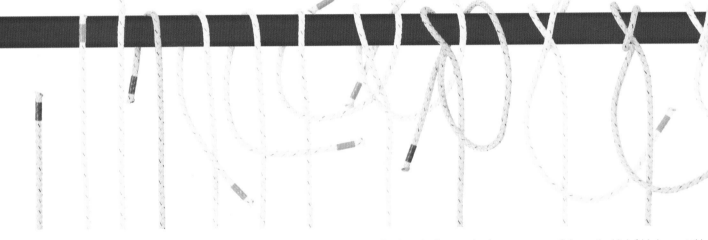

● Pass the working end of the line over the foundation rope or rail from the front to the back.

● Bring the working end up and across as if you were going to tie a simple clove hitch.

● When the first turn has been completed, make a second turn parallel with the first. So far the progress of this knot is exactly the same as if you were tying a traditional rolling hitch.

● Leave the hitch fairly loose at this stage so that it can be easily tightened when the hitch has been completed.

▶ **make a turn**

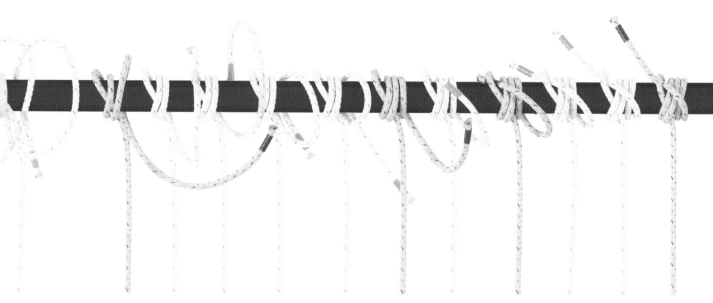

● The second turn is in place. You now take a third turn on the other side of the standing part of your rope. Here the turn is made to the right. The knot can be tied in either direction if wished.

● The third turn does not trap the standing part of the rope. When you have completed it, pull out a small bight in the standing part of your rope where it crosses the rail or foundation rope.

● Pass the working end over the three turns you have made and tuck the working end under this bight.

● Now, pull hard down on the standing part of your rope and the knot will be secure. This is a stronger knot than the rolling hitch, and the turns should be laid down in the direction of any lateral pull.

▶ **a second turn**　　▶ **a third turn the other side**　　▶ **back under the initial bight turn**

piwich knot

The Piwich knot was first introduced in 1995 in France, so named after a child of the Bois Brule Indian tribe who tied it.

It is a variant of the pedigree cow hitch. It is a simple knot that is often used to hang items on a lanyard or pole.

● Take the working end of the line around a pole or rail from the front to the back. This is not a particularly secure knot but is perfectly satisfactory when the strain is at right angles to the point of attachment.

● Take the working end out to the side. The first stage of the knot is to take a half hitch around the standing part of the line.

● The hitch can be tied either from right to left or from left to right, as shown here.

● Complete the half hitch by pulling the working part of your line through from left to right.

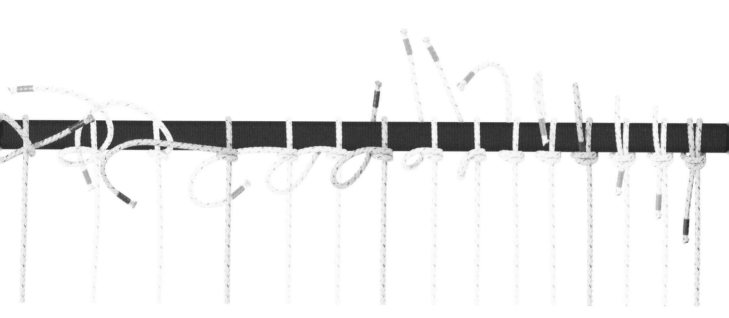

● Once you have made the half hitch, you then take the working end across the hitch in front of the standing part of your line.

● Pass the working part over the rail, this time from back to front. This is the opposite direction to the original turn around the rail.

● Complete the hitch by passing the working end down through the two loops you have formed. The working end and the standing part of the line lie parallel to each other, running down the front of the hitch.

● Tighten the hitch by pulling on both the standing part and working end of your line.

▶ **bring the line across**　　　▶　**then around the back**　　　▶　**down through both turns**　　**tighten**

mooring hitch

As its name implies, this hitch is usually used to secure small boats to mooring posts on the tideway. The drawloop is usually tied with a long end that is then led back to the boat, and any adjustment required by the rise and fall of the tide can be made from on board. The hitch is known as a "slide and lock knot."

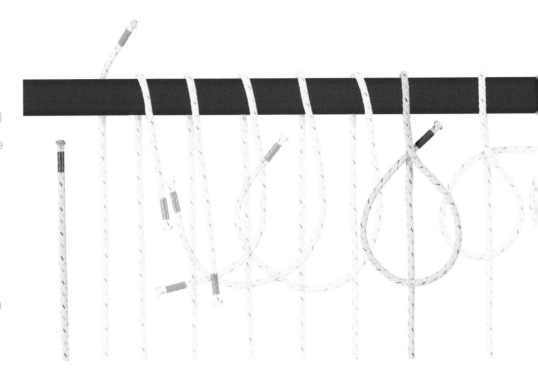

● Pass the line over the mooring post or rail from back to the front.

● Make an underhand loop with the working end of the line and place it on top of the standing part.

● It is important at this stage of tying the hitch to allow enough rope to make as large a bight as you require.

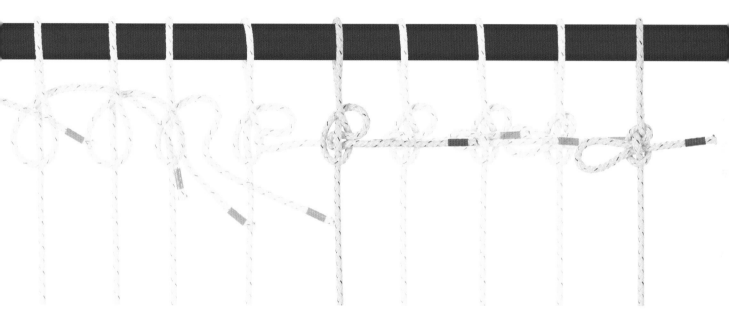

● The next stage of the hitch is to make a bight in the working end of the rope. Make sure that you have allowed enough rope to tie this part of the hitch easily.

● Push the bight over the nearest part of the loop, under the standing part of the line, and then over the second part of the loop. This over-under-over move is similar to that used when tying a carrick bend.

● The hitch is then tightened by pulling hard on the standing part of the rope. It is important to do this properly, particularly when securing boats on the tideway.

● If you need to lengthen the rope, pull on its short end to undo the hitch. Then retie the hitch as required.

make a bight　　　　　▶　　**the bight goes over-under-over**　　　　　▶　　**pull the standing line to tighten**

half blood knot

This is an extremely useful and popular knot that is mainly used by anglers to secure leaders to flies, lures, or swivels. If using fine nylon, it is important to moisten or lubricate the knot as it is tightened and to tighten the knot slowly because this makes it more secure. The knot is more secure if you take four or five turns around the standing part of the leader.

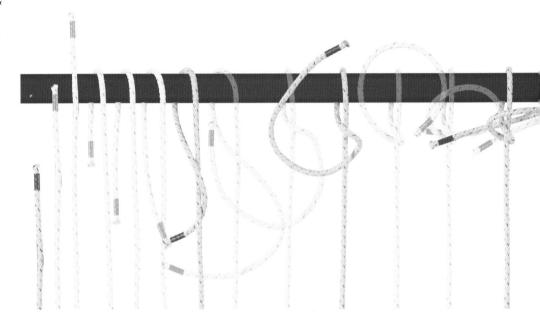

● As well as its common use by anglers to secure leaders to flies or lures, the half blood knot can also be used to secure a line to a post or hook. It can, however, be difficult to untie.

● Pass the line through the eye of the hook or around a rail as shown above. The tying method in this sequence is the same as for the full blood knot (see pages 32–33), working from the top down.

● Take the working end around the standing part of the line and make a series of neat coils, working down toward the point of attachment.

▶ **make a turn**

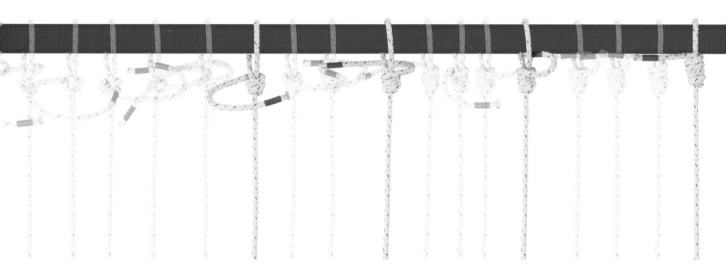

● In this sequence, three turns are taken. When tying this knot with fine monofilament, four or five turns are recommended to prevent the knot from slipping.

● The final turn is tucked through the loop formed by the standing part of the line and the last turn.

● Pull the working end of the line to tighten the last loop and then tighten the knot by pulling on the standing part of the line. When tied with fine monofilament, it is important to moisten or lubricate the knot.

● Both this and the full blood knot (see pages 32–33) can be tied the other way around: winding the turns up the standing part of the line rather than down and then bringing the working end down through the loop.

anchor bend

This knot is a close relative of the traditional round turn and two half hitches that many sailors use to secure ropes to mooring rings and posts. The anchor bend is more secure but a bit more complicated to tie. It is called, rather misleadingly, a bend rather than a hitch because old sailors always "bent" ropes to spars or anchors.

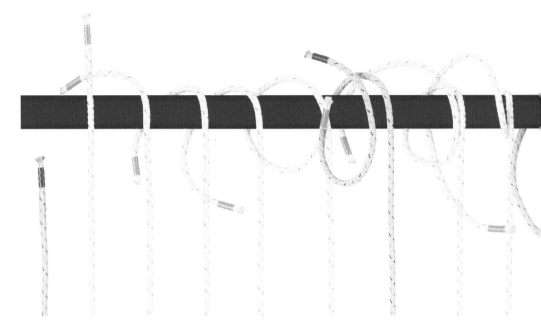

● The knot is normally tied to a ring. This sequence shows it tied to a rail. Make a round turn to start with.

● The working end of the rope goes over the rail twice. Both turns are made in the same direction, lie parallel to each other, and do not cross over.

● When the full round turn has been completed, take the working end of your rope across the front of the standing part of your line.

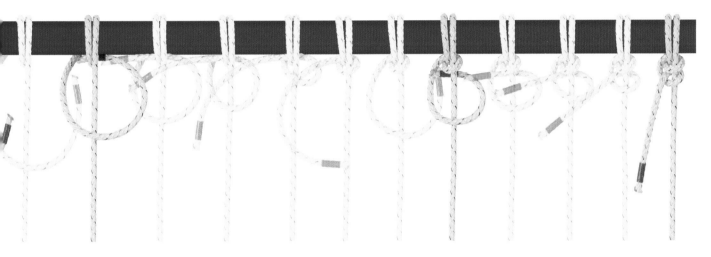

● Pass the working end through the round turn to tie a half hitch.

● The round turn traps the rope against the anchor ring or rail.

● The knot is then completed by adding another identical half hitch in the same direction as the first. This second half hitch does not pass under the round turn.

● If the anchor bend is intended as a permanent or semi-permanent hitch, then you should leave a long working end that can be taped or whipped to the standing part of your rope.

cat's paw

This is a hitch tied "in the bight" to lessen the strain that a heavy load would put on a single line. It was employed by the stevedores when handling heavy loads using hooks.

● Start by making a large bight in a long length of line or double a rope.

● Take hold of the top of the bight and pull it toward you, making the two "eyes" or loops shown in the sequence above.

● Pull the bight down until the loops are large enough for the number of twists that you plan to insert.

● Twist the two loops in opposite directions. In this instance, the left-hand loop is twisted counterclockwise, the right-hand loop clockwise. Another way of remembering is to twist each loop from inside to outside.

■   ▶ **make a bight**   ▶ **pull the top down**   ▶ **twist**

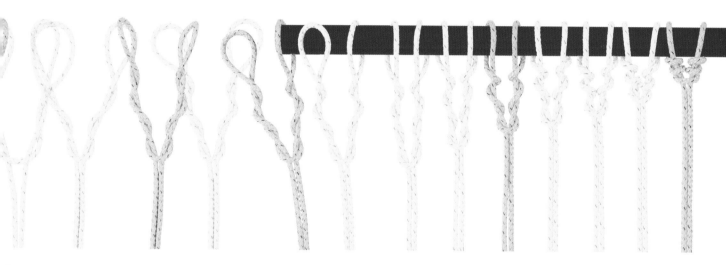

● It is usual to insert three or four twists. Each loop must have identical numbers.

● Insert the hook or anchorage point through the top of both loops. Here, the loops are replaced on the rail, but it is much easier just to slip them on to a hook.

● Pull evenly on both standing parts of the line and then slide the knot as close to the attachment point as possible.

● Using a cat's paw is a security measure when hoisting heavy loads— for if one strand of the rope breaks, the other may hold the load long enough for it be be lowered to the ground without damage.

gaff topsail halyard bend

This simple hitch was originally used to secure the topsail along the gaff of a sailing ship. Nowadays gaff-rigged ships are comparative rarities. The knot is more secure than it appears and can be used anywhere that requires a simple and effective hitch. Its other advantage is that it can virtually be tied with one hand, hence its popularity on sailing ships.

● Pass the rope over the beam as shown, bringing the end toward you. Allow enough rope to make two turns over the beam, as well as the finishing hitch. You may need more rope than you might think.

● Pass the bight of rope to your left. If necessary you can do this using one hand only. Pull all the rope you require over the beam toward you.

● Take the bight of rope back over the beam, to the left of the standing part of the rope, laying down two parallel turns, side by side. The second turn is made to the left of the first.

▶ **make one turn**

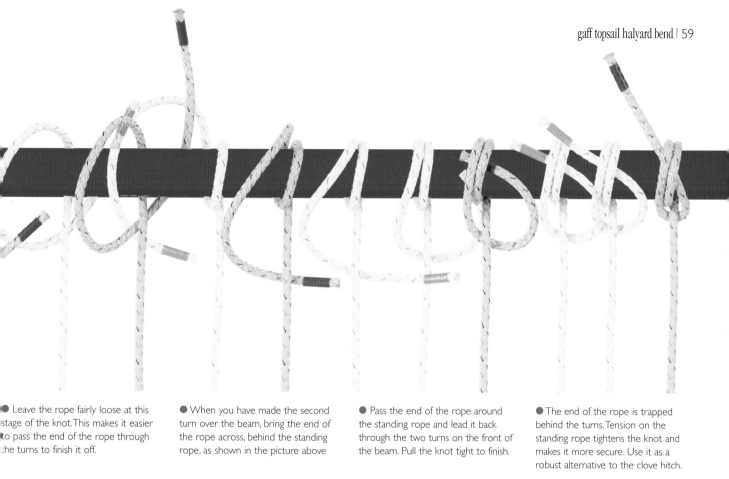

● Leave the rope fairly loose at this stage of the knot. This makes it easier to pass the end of the rope through the turns to finish it off.

● When you have made the second turn over the beam, bring the end of the rope across, behind the standing rope, as shown in the picture above

● Pass the end of the rope around the standing rope and lead it back through the two turns on the front of the beam. Pull the knot tight to finish.

● The end of the rope is trapped behind the turns. Tension on the standing rope tightens the knot and makes it more secure. Use it as a robust alternative to the clove hitch.

buntline hitch

Buntlines were attached to the foot-rope of sails to prevent them bellying out when they were being furled. They were used on the square sails of ships-of-the-line. It was important that the knot used did not shake loose, so the buntline hitch was devised with this in mind. The knot is essentially two half hitches, one tied inside the other. It is the same knot as a four-in-hand necktie.

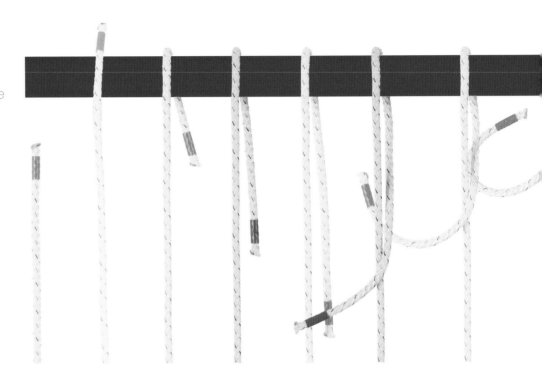

● Take the working end of the line around or through the point of attachment from front to back.

● The knot can be tied in either direction. Here the working end has been taken out to the right.

● Take a complete turn around the standing part of the line. If using the hitch as a stopping knot, do not make the knot with more line than necessary.

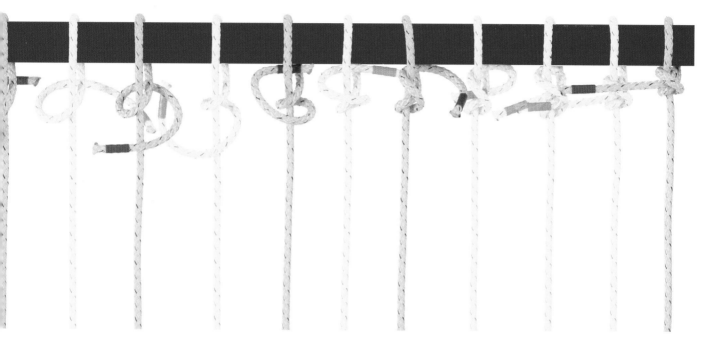

● The first part of the hitch is a figure-of-eight made around the standing part. This makes the first half hitch of the knot

● When the figure-of-eight is completed, the working end of the line goes through the loop nearest the point of attachment from left to right. This is the opposite direction to the initial direction of the working end.

● It is a help to leave the knot reasonably loose at this stage so that the second half hitch can be completed and the length of the working end adjusted if necessary.

● Finish the hitch by taking the working end back through the bight of the line formed by the first half hitch, from right to left as shown. Bed the knot down neatly. This makes a secure knot that will not come loose.

figure-of-eight ▶ **through the loop** ▶ **take under and tighten** ■

loops

figure-of-eight loop

In the past, sailors called this knot the Flemish loop, but it was never popular at sea because it tended to jam when wet and tied in manilla or hemp cordage. Today, it is frequently used by climbers because it is easily tied and can be checked by the team leader, even in the poorest light. It can be used by anglers to tie a loop at the end of a leader.

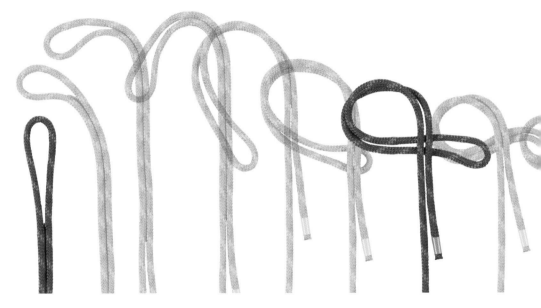

● Make a large bight at the end of your line or rope. As with most loops, this is easier to tie if you give yourself plenty of rope to work with.

● Make a loop with the bight as shown above and take it underneath the standing and working ends of your line. There are several different methods of tying this loop but this is one of the easiest.

● Take the bight across to form a loop in the line. The figure-of-eight is made by bringing the loop back over the top of the working and standing lines.

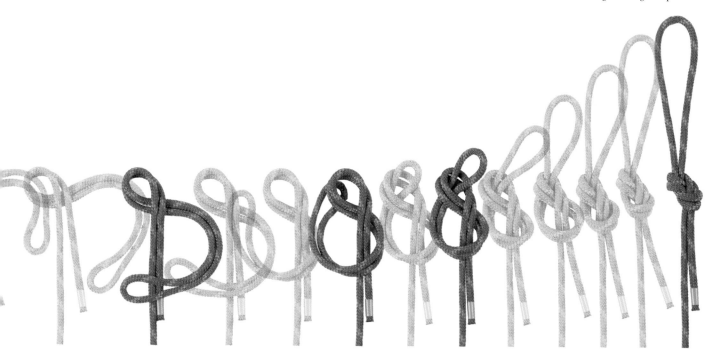

● An alternative method is to make two half twists in the original bight, one after the other. This produces the figure-of-eight.

● Take the end of the bight around, under and through the loop you have made in the line. This completes the knot.

● Pull the loop through and bed the knot down so that the loop is firm, neat, and tight.

● If you wish, you can secure the working end to the standing part of the line with two half hitches. This provides additional security in the unlikely event of the loop slipping under any sudden strain.

▶ **around and through**　　　　　　▶ **tighten**

loops

bowline

This time-honored knot does not slip, loosen, or jam. Sailors were taught to tie it around their waists with their eyes shut so that if they were washed overboard and thrown a line, they could secure the line with a bowline and be pulled back on board. As its name implies, it was originally the line that led from the bow of a sailing ship to the weather leech of a square sail.

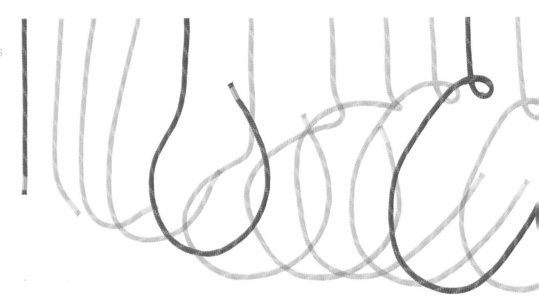

● There are a number of mnemonics that help the beginner to tie this knot correctly. The best known probably is: "the rabbit puts his head out of the hole, goes around the tree, and back down the hole again."

● The first step when tying the knot is to make the rabbit's hole. Make a large bight in the line and then place your hand at the standing end of the bight. Give the rope a half twist to make a smaller loop.

● The standing part of the line must be on the underneath. Take the working end of the line, the rabbit, and lead it through the loop from the back to the front.

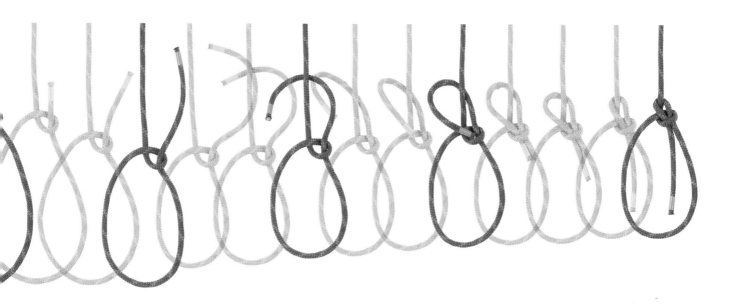

● An alternative method of doing this is to place the working end across, nd on top of, the standing part, orming a large bight, and then turn he line over with a half twist.

● This makes the small loop and brings the working end of the line into the correct position in one movement. Take the working end around behind the standing part of the line.

● Finish the knot by taking the working end back down through the small loop. The standing part of the line is "the tree," and the small loop is "the rabbit's hole."

● Pull the knot tight. It will not slip and can be used as a loop when tying parcels or during tree surgery.

loops

water bowline

This is another version of the ordinary bowline, which is supposedly less likely to jam when wet than the traditional version shown on pages 66–67. A good secure knot, it is more difficult to tie than the ordinary bowline, which has the advantage that it can be tied freehand under all circumstances.

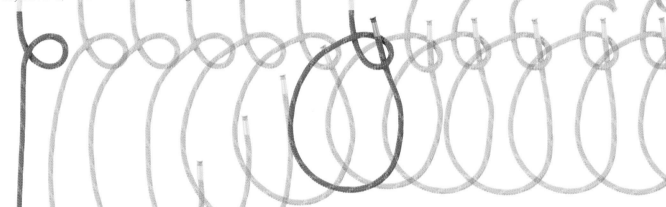

● Either start by making a small loop as shown above or follow the first steps of tying the traditional bowline on page 66.

● Take the working end of the line around, making a large bight. Lead the end through the small loop from the back to the front.

● Make a second loop in the standing part of the line identical to, and just above, the first loop. It is easiest to do this on a flat surface.

● Take the end of the line through this second loop in the same way as the first. The end must go through the loop from the back to the front.

▶ make a small underhand loop ▶ make a bight ▶ up through ▶

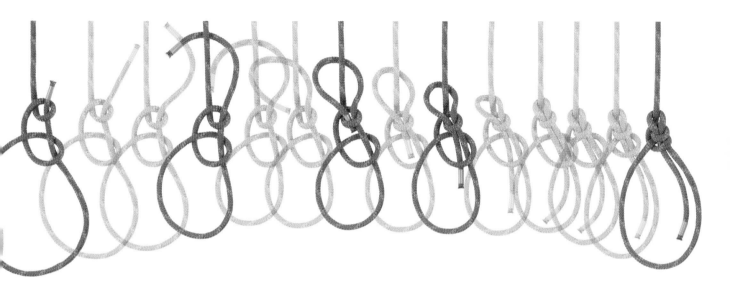

● Keeping the loops fairly open, take the working end of the line around behind the standing part.

● Then take the end down through both loops so that it lies parallel to its own standing part.

● Tighten the knot. You may find that you have to pull the lower loop up so that it lies snugly against the knot.

● This knot withstands rougher handling than an ordinary bowline, but it is not used so frequently.

another underhand loop ▶ **through again** ▶ **tighten**

loops
perfection loop

This knot used to be called the angler's loop and was commonly used in the 17th century when anglers fished with gut and horsehair lines. Today, it is most often used as a secure knot that can even be tied in bungee (elasticated) lines. It can also be tied in the bight, which many people find easier and quicker, but this method is easier to learn.

● The first step when tying this knot is to make an overhand knot with a drawloop.

● Make a large bight in the line or rope. The standing part of the line goes over the working end as shown.

● Make a second loop. The working end is brought back over the first loop, making two loops that look like a pair of spectacles.

● Pull the second loop down through the first. This may look complicated, but it is quite simple in practice.

● The first stage of the knot is now complete. At this stage, the knot is a simple overhand knot with a drawloop. The working end and the standing part of the line lie parallel to each other.

● To finish the knot, take the working end of the line around the back of the standing part and then back through the center of the knot, trapping it beneath the two legs of the loop

● Pull the knot tight. This simple-looking knot makes a surprisingly secure loop.

▶ **pull it through**   ▶ **around behind**   ▶ **across and tighten**

alpine butterfly

This well-known European mountaineering knot is used to secure middlemen on a line. Its other name is the linesman's loop. John Street, who wrote the classic book on scouting ropework, called it the "queen of knots." Like all the best knots, it is secure, and easy to tie. It is always tied in the bight—a necessity for knots of this purpose.

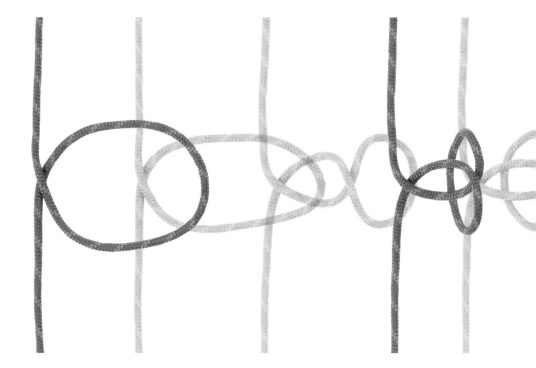

● Make a large loop in the line. The top part of the line lies over the top of the lower part.

● Pull the loop out to elongate it and make a half twist with the top of the loop coming over the bottom. The loop is now a figure-of-eight.

● Bring the front part of the figure-of-eight back behind itself to make the rope into a heart shape.

● Pick up the bottom of the heart and form it into a loop. Push this loop through the center of the loop at the top of the knot.

● Pull the loop through to make a large bight in the line. It is a good idea to make the initial loop fairly large as, this way, it is easier to make the finished loop the size you wish.

● As you tighten the knot, you create two smaller loops at each side with the larger loop at the tail as shown above. This gives the knot its characteristic butterfly appearance.

● Tighten the knot securely. There are many ways to to tie this knot, but this is the simplest and easiest to learn.

loops

double figure-of-eight loop

This is the double looped version of the popular climber's knot. The loops can be adjusted

to differing sizes if required. It is quite secure and is always tied in the bight.

● Make a large bight in a length of rope. Then, make a loop in the bight by taking a half twist in a clockwise direction.

● Now, take the loop and end bight up and across the two standing parts of the line.

● At the same time, make another clockwise half twist in the standing ends of the line. This makes two double loops to the right, with the original single loop on the left of the two standing parts of the line.

● Take the standing ends through the single loop leading them through from the back to the front. Take the right hand double loop through the left hand double loop as shown.

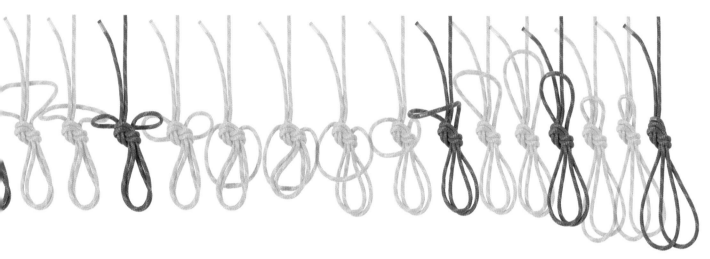

● It is very important that they are brought through from the back to the front. In effect, this makes a doubled figure-of-eight knot. It is difficult to do at first, and you may have to practice it before you can tie it perfectly.

● Take the single loop at the top of the knot down and around the doubled loops to complete the knot.

● The knot is tied with this loop taken around both standing parts of the line.

● Pull on both loops to tighten the knot neatly and finish.

make an overhand knot ▶ **bring the single loop under and around** ▶ **tighten to secure**

loops

bowline in the bight

This traditional knot was used when transferring personnel from ship to ship at sea when two loops were required. It can be tied in a number of ways, but this method is done in the bight.

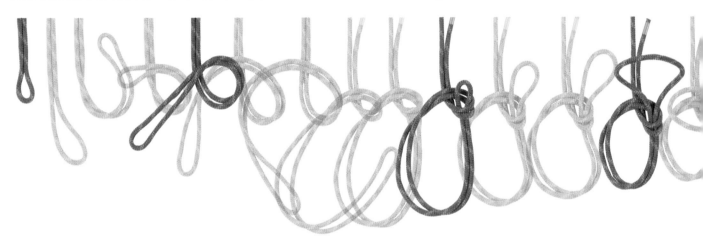

● Make a large bight in your rope or center it. Make a small loop with the standing parts of the bight on the underneath as if you were about to tie a double-stranded bowline.

● Bring the loop around in the bight and take it through the small loop, from back to front. This is exactly the same as if you were tying an ordinary bowline with a doubled rope.

● Pull the loop through to make a large bight in the line. The knot is easier to tie if you are generous with the amount of rope at this stage.

● Bring the standing parts of the rope through this loop from the back to the front as shown.

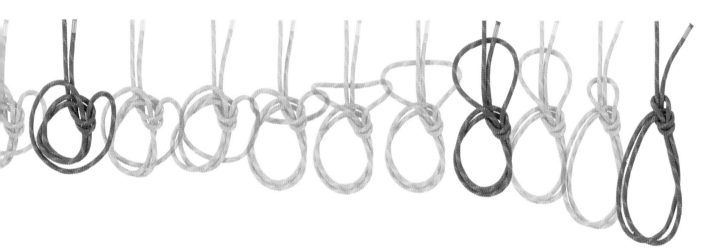

● Bring the loop down and pass the whole knot through it from underneath.

● Take the loop back up to the top of the knot. Take the two standing parts of the rope through as before, working from the front to the back.

● This traps the two loops securely. Pull down on the knot to tighten it. This is a simpler method of making two loops in a rope than the double figure-of-eight loop (see pages 74–75).

● The triple bowline (see pages 78–79) and Portuguese bowline are further developments from the traditional "king of knots."

triple bowline

This is a simpler knot to tie than the bowline in the bight. It was devised by Robert Chisnall, the Canadian mountaineer, to allow a beginner and an instructor to belay at the same point with a secure loop for each. The knot, in essence, is an ordinary bowline tied in the bight, with the last loop forming the triple part of the knot.

● Make a large bight in a rope and make a small loop with the standing part of the bight on the underneath.

● Take the end of the bight around, making as large loop as required. This forms the two main loops of the knot.

● Then, take the end of the bight through the small loop from the back to the front just as if you were tying a single bowline.

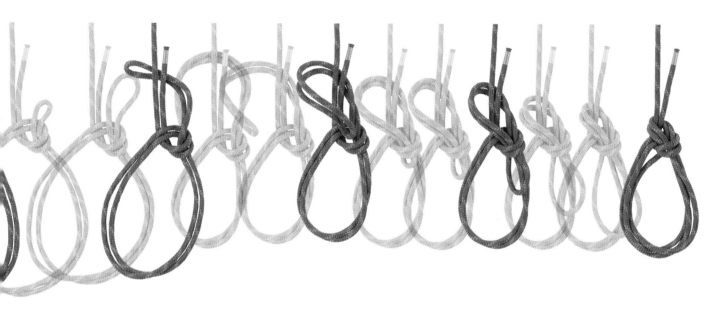

● Pass the loop around the back of the standing parts of the line. Make sure that you have allowed enough rope so that you make three good-sized loops.

● Then, take the loop back down through the original loop.

● Ease the loop down until you have three loops of the required size.

● Tighten the knot by taking three loops in one hand and the two standing parts of the line in the other. Pull them apart to tighten. If one of the standing parts is short, you can secure it with two half hitches.

scaffold knot

The scaffold knot makes a strong, secure sliding loop that, no doubt, was used for executions in the days when the purpose of a public hanging was to draw out the agonies of the condemned prisoner for the delight of the crowd. The knot would gradually tighten and strangle the victim. Today, it is used instead of an eye splice by sailors to hold metal or plastic liners, called thimbles.

● With a little practice, this simple knot can be tied in 10 seconds, which makes it very useful for tying parcels and around the home.

● Make a bight at the end of a line or piece of rope and take the working end across and around the back of the standing part as shown.

● Bring the working end across to the front and then around the back of both parts of the loop.

● Tuck the end through in a figure-of-eight, as shown, trapping the standing part of the loop.

● Take the working end up through the first loop as shown. This traps the knot securely.

● Pull on the end and the appropriate part of the loop in opposite directions to tighten the knot securely.

● You now have a strong slip knot that will not come undone under any normal strain or circumstances. Multiple scaffold knots are stronger and may be used to withstand greater loads.

figure-of-eight behind   ▶   **through both loops**   ▶   **tighten**

loops
tarbuck knot

This versatile, general-purpose knot was named after climber Ken Tarbuck,

who popularized it when nylon climbing ropes were first adopted (about 1952).

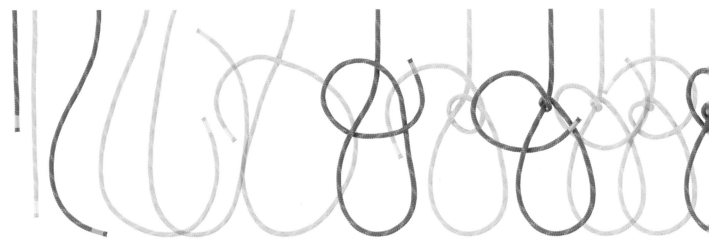

● Slide-and-grip knots are designed to give to start with, but then to grip as the strain on the line increases. This knot was first used by American lumberjacks.

● Make a loop with the working end of your line about the size you wish. Take the working end down and around behind the loop that you have formed.

● Complete the first wrapping turn and then make a second wrapping turn around the loop parallel with the first.

● Both these turns are made in the same direction. When the second turn has been completed take the working end of the line up around the standing part of the line, above the loop that you have formed.

● This turn goes over the top of the first two turns and around behind the standing part as shown.

● Bring the end back to the front and then tuck the end through itself from right to left.

● This last turn forms a figure-of-eight around the standing part of the line. Pull the end through in order to tighten the knot.

● The knot is now complete. When placed under sudden strain, the knot makes a dog's leg in the standing part of the line and the loop will not close.

▶ **then a turn above**　　　　▶ **around, through, down and tighten**

chair knot

The chair knot, or fireman's chair knot, is designed to lower anyone trapped in a building or on a cliff: one loop goes under the arms and the other under the knees. The rescuer lowers the victim with one rope while a second rescuer pulls them away from a wall with the other.

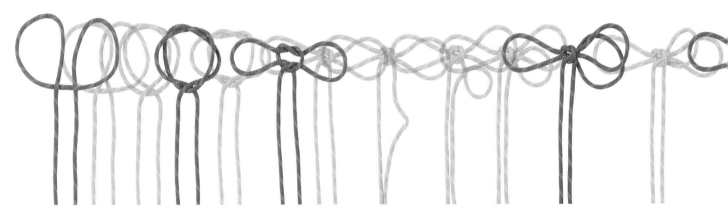

● Make a clockwise overhand loop in the bight of the rescue rope and then add a counterclockwise underhand loop on the right of the first loop. Make both loops the same size.

● Overlap the two loops with the right hand loop in front. Pull the leading edge of both loops through the opposite loop; the right-hand loop from the back to the front and the left-hand loop from front to back.

● This makes a bow with two loops on either side as shown. Pull the ends of each loop to tighten the knot you have formed.

● Form a loop in the standing part of each line by making a half twist, clockwise with the left-hand line and counterclockwise with the right. Do these one at a time.

make two loops   ▶   **pull them through each other**   ▶   **make a half hitch**

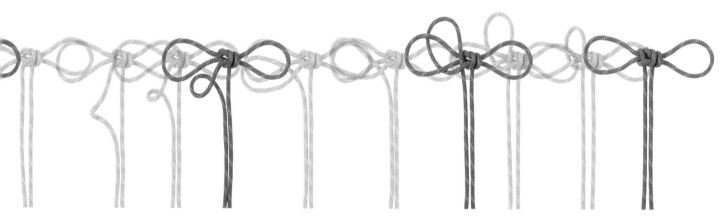

● Pass the loops through the smaller loops you have just made in the standing part of each line. In effect, you are tying a half hitch around the two main loops.

● Do this with one standing rope and then the other. Here, the right line has been knotted before the left.

● Adjust each large loop to the required size; then tighten the standing lines firmly, one at a time. This beds down the half hitches and makes the loops secure.

● Throw one of the standing ropes to the second rescuer on the ground. Place the two loops round the victim's knees and armpits, and lower away.

▷ **take it over and tighten**　　　▷ **repeat the other side**　　　▷ **pull tight to finish**

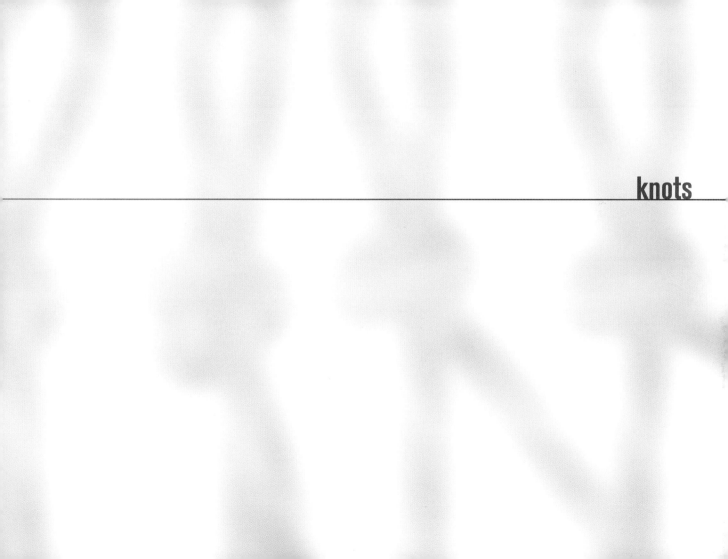

knots

knots

ashley's (or oysterman's) stopper knot

Stopper knots are tied at the ends of lines, such as sheets or halyards, to prevent the working ends unreeving from their shackles. They are also used in the home, for example when tying parcels, to stop line running through a loop when sewing, and when trussing joints of meat. The simplest stopper knot is the simple overhand or thumb knot.

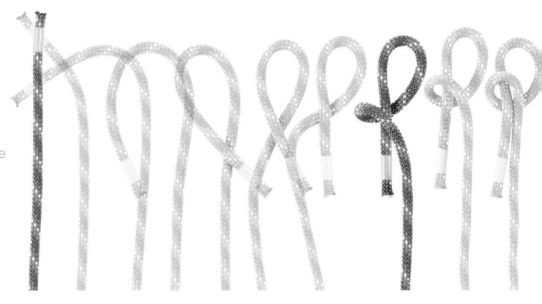

● While the thumb knot will suffice as a stopper knot on many occasions, it is better to get into the habit of tying this stopper knot because it provides greater bulk and security. It can also be undone easily.

● First of all, tie an overhand, or thumb, knot with the addition of a drawloop. Here, the knot is tied as one, but you can tie a simple overhand knot and then lead one end back through, if you prefer.

● Take the standing part of the rope around the back of the working end and then take a bight up through the loop you have formed.

▶   make a drawloop

● Pull the loop through. The working end and standing part of the line lie parallel with each other.

● Pull the loop reasonably tight but do not tighten the knot completely at this stage.

● Take the working end and bring it back through the loop as shown. When you pull on the standing part of the line, the loop will bite down on the working end, trapping it at the top of the knot.

● This makes a secure, relatively bulky stopping knot that will not come loose under normal conditions.

▶ **pull through**　　　　　　　　▶ **take the end through**　　　▶ **tighten**

prusik knot

This knot was invented by Dr. Karl Prusik, an Austrian music professor who devised it during the First World War to mend the broken strings of musical instruments. He later published a book showing how it could be adapted for mountaineering. It was one of the first slide-and-grip knots that are now all referred to as prusiking knots.

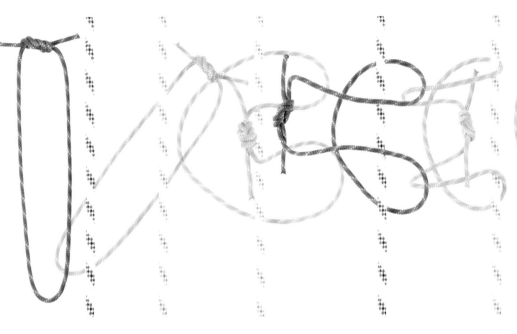

● The Prusik knot is used to secure a stirrup sling to a climbing rope. The knot jams under strain and holds firm, but when the weight is removed, the knot comes free and can be pushed up or down the rope.

● The climbing rope in the diagram is on the right; the stirrup is the purple rope on the left. Loop the stirrup over the rope and pull it down through itself. This makes the first two loops round the rope.

● Take the stirrup round again in the same direction; make another loop and pull it down.

▶ **loop the sling over the climbing rope**

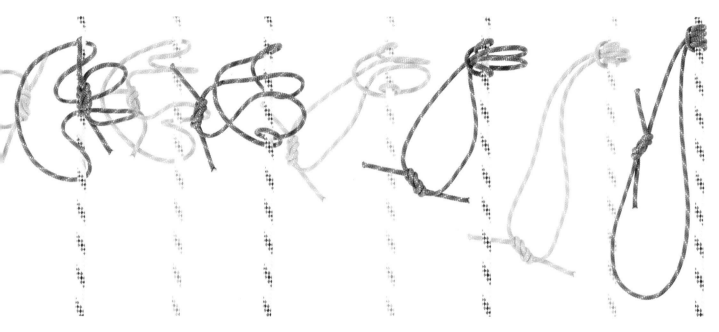

● You may be able to tie the knot as shown above, or you can make a bight with the stirrup over the climbing rope and feed the stirrup through. The end result is exactly the same.

● Pull the end of the stirrup down. You now have four turns around the climbing rope. If the turns are left loose at this stage, they can be pushed up and down the rope.

● Here the turns have been pushed as far up the rope as possible before tightening. The knot will now take your weight. Climbers can maneuver their way up a rope using two stirrups attached by Prusik knots.

● In wet or icy conditions, you can wrap the stirrup around once or twice more for extra security, giving you six or eight turns. This creates a double or triple Prusik knot.

▶ **make another loop**　　　　▶ **pull down to tighten**

frost knot

The Frost knot was invented in the 1960s by Tom Frost, a noted mountaineer. Although the knot is shown here tied in cord, it was designed to be tied in webbing. It is used when improvising short lengths of climbing ladders, called étriers, from the French word for stirrups. When tied in webbing, the knot should be kept as flat as possible.

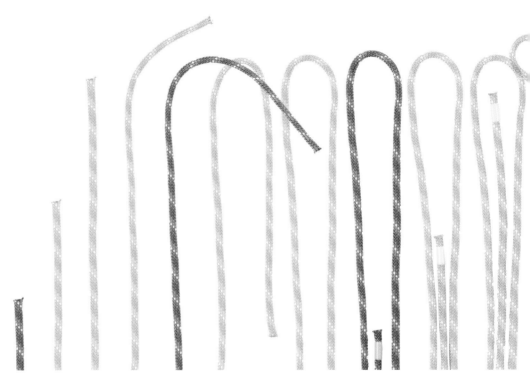

● The Frost knot is simplicity itself. The arrangement of the length of the rope, or webbing, means that the end knot creates two loops, one at each end that can then be used by mountaineers.

● Make a bight in one end of your line and then bring the other end up in the middle of the bight.

● This produces three lengths of line, with one working end in the middle of the bight at the top and the other working end to the side of the second bight at the bottom. This is not shown in the diagram above.

● Take the bight down and make an counterclockwise loop with all three parts, as shown above.

● Take the bight and the extra end around behind the loop and pull it through carefully. In effect, you are tying a simple overhand knot with all three parts of the line.

● Be sure that all the parts are together before tightening the knot. When the knot is completed, you have two loops; in this case you have one small one at the top and a larger one at the foot.

● When using webbing, keep all the parts together so that the strands are level and lie one on top of each other. You can vary the size of the loop, depending on the length of the rope and where you tie your knot.

bachmann knot

This knot is used with a karabiner and can be moved up and down a climbing rope more easily that the original Prusik knot. It relies on the friction between the sling, the karabiner, and climbing rope to hold it in place. It can easily be released when the tension is removed from the sling.

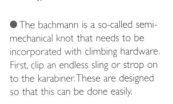

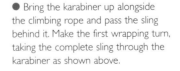

● The bachmann is a so-called semi-mechanical knot that needs to be incorporated with climbing hardware. First, clip an endless sling or strop on to the karabiner. These are designed so that this can be done easily.

● Bring the karabiner up alongside the climbing rope and pass the sling behind it. Make the first wrapping turn, taking the complete sling through the karabiner as shown above.

● Pull the turn tight to bring the karabiner into close contact with the climbing rope. Keep the ropes of the sling even and ensure that they lie parallel with each other.

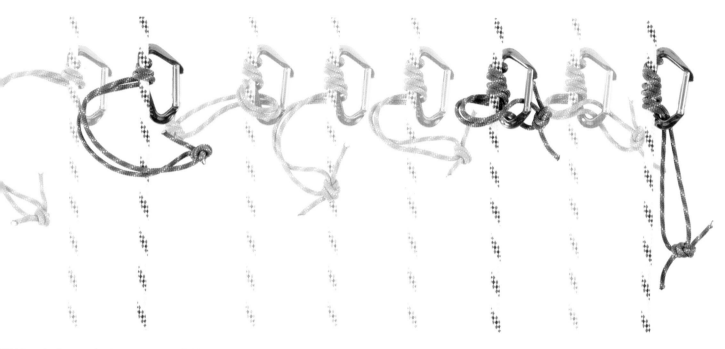

● When the first turn has been completed, take another wrapping turn through the karabiner.

● Make sure that the turns lie evenly and that they are kept close to one another.

● Lay down wrapping turns until the karabiner is full. Resist the temptation to fill it too full. Three turns, as shown here, are normally sufficient. The wrapping turns hold the karabiner in place on the climbing rope.

● When any weight is placed on the sling, the friction jams it in place. If the weight is released, the sling can be moved up and down the rope easily.

▶ **and two more**　　　　　　　　　▶ **pull the sling down**

klemheist knot

This is another friction hitch used by mountaineers. It can also be tied around a karabiner, which makes it easier to move up and down. The knot is normally tied with four or five turns taken around the climbing rope instead of the three illustrated here; this makes it more secure.

As with all prusiking knots, the diameter of the rope used for the sling must be less than the rope itself.

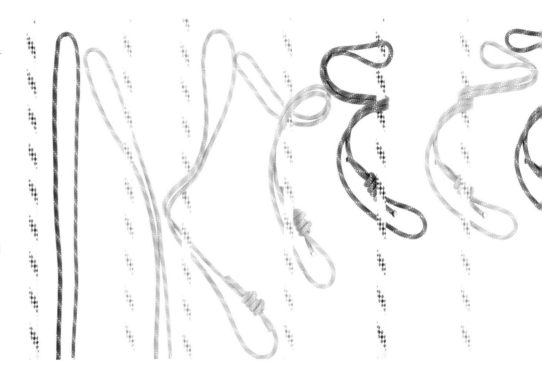

● Take the top bight in a sling and start to wrap it around the climbing rope. Always wrap in an upward direction, the opposite way to the direction of the strain on the knot when it is loaded.

● Continue to wrap the sling, making sure that each turn lies neatly parallel to the one below and that there are no crossovers.

● Here, the first turn has been completed and the second turn has been started. It is important to untwist any crossovers as they develop.

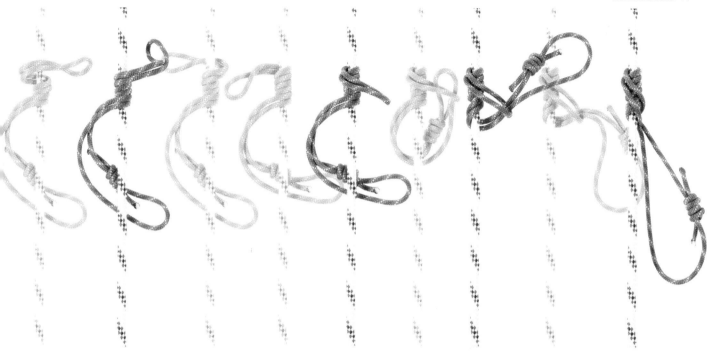

● Lay down a third turn and then bring the top bight down to complete the knot. Extra turns are often used at this point for additional security, particularly in muddy or icy conditions—which make the ropes slippery.

● The top bight comes over the turns you have laid down, and the standing part of the sling is then brought up and passed through the top bight.

● This secures the knot. Make sure that the top bight is long enough to lie neatly over the turns.

● The principle behind this knot is the same as the traditional rolling hitch that resists any pull in a lateral direction. It is more secure that the Prusik knot and slightly easier to tie.

▶ **take three turns**   ▶ **pass the bottom loop through the top loop**   ▶ **tighten**

penberthy knot

This is another prusiking knot that does not have to be tied in the bight. Therefore, a long length of rope can be used. It is a caver's knot and is sometimes called the caver's helical knot.

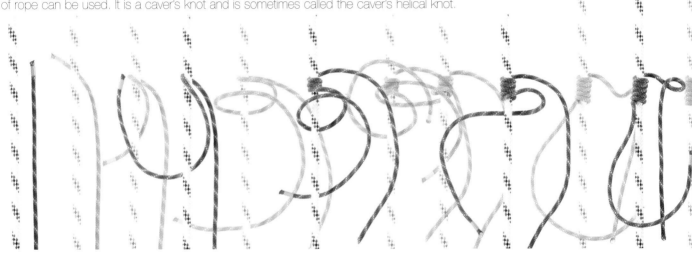

● This knot was developed by Larry Penberthy and Dick Mitchell in the late 1960s. Start by selecting a rope of suitable diameter and lay it next to the climbing rope.

● Wind a number of turns around the climbing rope. These can be wound either up the climbing rope or down, as shown here. Adjust the number of turns required and the amount of slack to the weight of the user.

● Make sure that the turns are even and lie neatly together. Four or five turns are sufficient under ordinary circumstances.

● To secure the knot, make an overhand loop in the upper of the two cords as shown above.

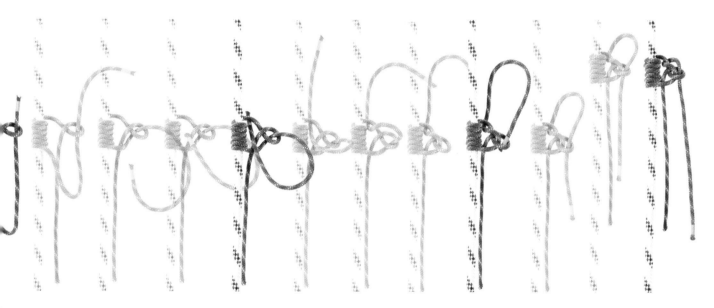

● The loop is now used to tie a sheet bend around the upper cord with the lower one. Take the lower of the two cords and lead it through the loop from the bottom to the top as shown.

● Pass the working end of the lower cord around the back of the top of the loop formed by the upper cord. If you think of tying a sheet bend (see pages 24–25), finishing the knot becomes easier.

● Bring the cord back down through the loop to finish the knot; this forms a sheet bend.

● Pull on the end of the cord to tighten the knot and then lower the long end down to any caver who may be in difficulties underground.

▶ **tie a sheet bend**

▶ **tighten** ■

double munter friction hitch

The double munter friction hitch was developed by Robert Chisnall as a variation on the original hitch. The hitch provides added friction, which gives the climber more control over the load line.

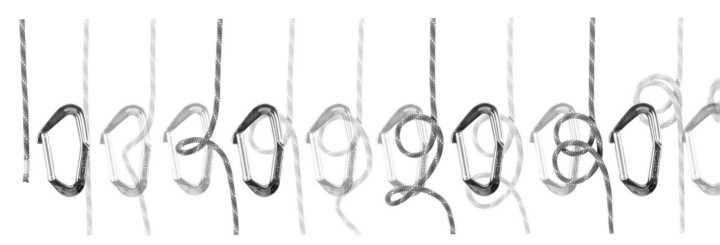

- The original knot provided climbers with an effective means of abseiling (rappelling), belaying, or absorbing the energy of a fall. When first introduced, it was also called the Italian hitch or sliding ring hitch.

- The double munter friction hitch includes an additional turn around the karabiner, which creates greater friction and, therefore, more control. It is ideal for rope of small diameter.

- To start, take two turns in the climbing rope and place them side by side forming a double loop.

- Open the karabiner and take the standing end of the climbing rope through the karabiner from the back to the front. This must be done correctly or the hitch will not work.

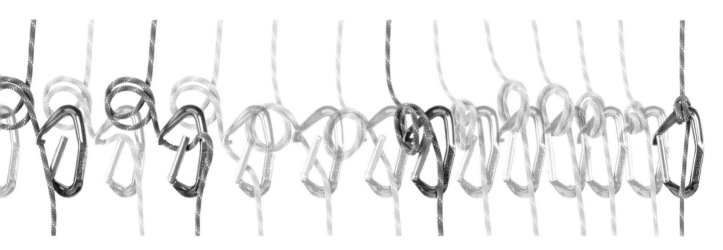

● Then, pass the karabiner through the double loop, again from back to front. As before, this must be done correctly or the hitch will not work.

● The effect of this is to bring the lower standing part of the climbing rope over the two hitches. Any downward pressure on the rope then presses the loops against the karabiner, creating friction.

● As the friction increases, the knot will eventually lock up and any falling climber will be brought to a halt. It is not generally used for abseiling (rappelling), as it causes synthetic ropes to overheat and glaze sheath filaments.

● When the loops are in place, the karabiner is closed; the finished hitch is shown above.

▶ **standing end through the karabiner**　　　▶　**clip on the loops**　　　▶　**pull down**

sheepshank

The sheepshank is used to shorten a rope temporarily, without the need to cut it—as well as to bridge a weakened section of rope—by taking any strain upon the two other parts of the knot. It is the basis for a bellringer's knot, keeping ropes suspended above the belfry floor when not in use, and forms the hitch used by truckers to tension and lash down lorry loads.

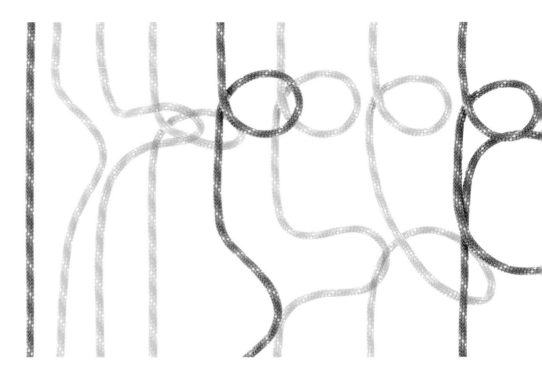

● There are numerous sheepshank knots, but the one shown here is the most convenient to learn and tie. Apply it in all sorts of situations. The uses to which it can be put are—like the method of tying—endless.

● Make a small loop in one of the standing parts of the rope. Here, the first loop has been made at the top of the line in a clockwise direction.

● Then, make a large loop—the amount that you wish to shorten the rope by—in the center of the rope. This loop is made counterclockwise.

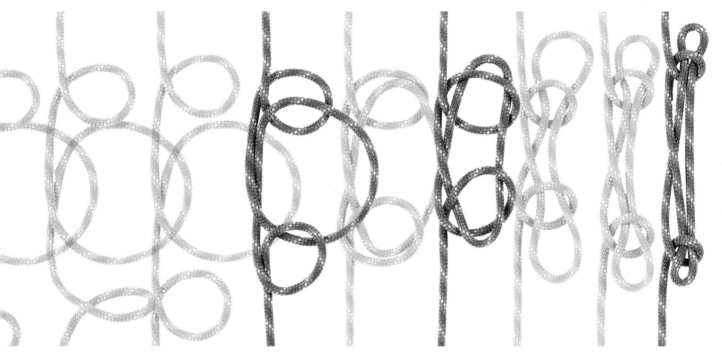

● Now, make a third loop, also counterclockwise, in the other standing part of the line. You now have three loops, one large and two small. The large loop in the center forms a double bight.

● Each end of the double bight is then pushed through the loops, the top from front to back and the bottom from back to front.

● Finally, pull on both standing parts of the rope to tighten the knot.

● With the sheepshank, it is advisable to take care of it between tying it and using it; otherwise, it will fall apart easily.

slide and cling hitch

This is another Robert Chisnall invention and is designed for mountaineers. The webbing extends under loading, which reduces its diameter, and then clings to the climbing rope. Its slide, grip, and hold characteristics make it ideal for climbers. The tape works equally well on double or single climbing ropes.

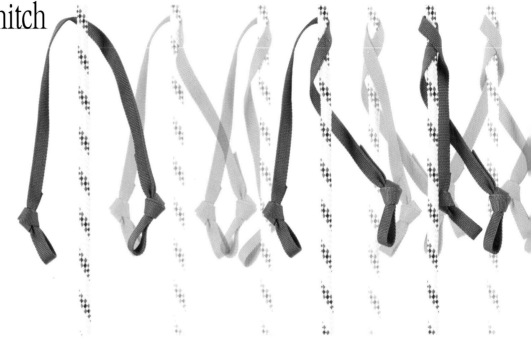

● First of all, tie two figure-of-eight loops at each end of the tape through which you can pass a karabiner to finish off the knot.

● Through the middle the tape pass a bight around the climbing rope. Then, start to wrap the tape around the rope, taking each end in opposite directions. Cross the tape over itself neatly, both front and back.

● To ensure that the friction is evenly distributed when the tape is placed under a shock load, make sure that the tapes pass over and under each other alternately. This is clearly shown in the diagrams and is very important.

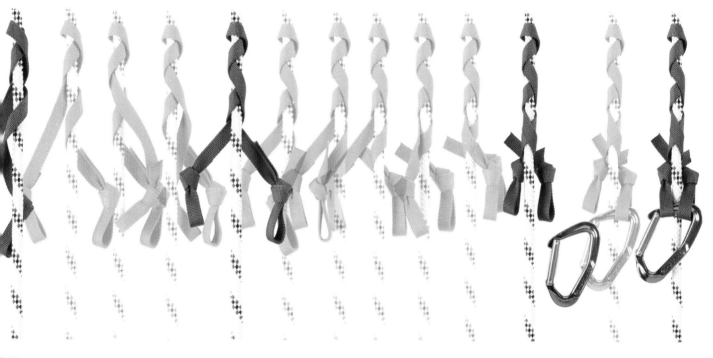

● The best method of ensuring this is to make alternate turns with each length of tape. Keep the turns as close together as possible.

● Try to make the diamonds between the tapes as small and regular as possible. Take eight or ten turns around the rope if possible. This will ensure that the knot holds properly.

● Finish off with the two figure-of-eight loops as close to the climbing rope as you can manage. Bring them both around to one side.

● Secure the knot by passing a karabiner through both loops and closing it securely. Attach a weighted line or climbing harness to this.

▶ **take eight or nine turns**

▶ **secure with a karabiner**

knots

eskimo bowline

The Eskimo bowline was discovered by Geoffrey Budworth (in 1985). It was tied on an Inuit (Eskimo) sled that was given as a gift to the Arctic explorer Sir John Ross, who then brought it back to England in the 19th century. The sled can currently be seen in the Museum of Mankind, London. It contains a large number of such knots, all tied in rawhide lashings.

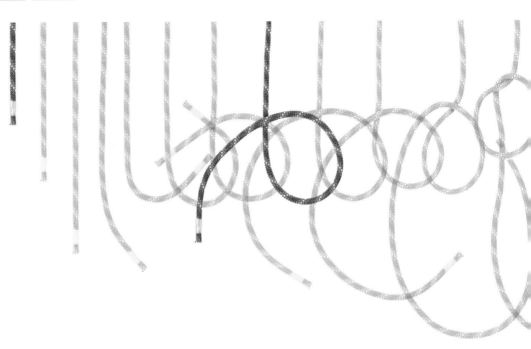

● The Eskimo bowline is more secure than the ordinary bowline, especially when tied with synthetic line. Once mastered, it is easy to tie.

● Make a large bight in a line the same size that you require your finished loop to be.

● Make a loop at the top of the bight with the working end of the line hanging down at the back. This is an incomplete overhand knot, or marlinspike hitch.

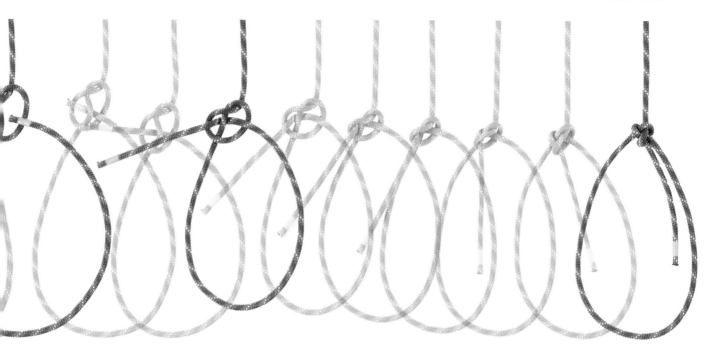

● Bring the end of the working line over the loop and secure it by passing it through the marlinspike hitch in an an over-under-over manner as shown.

● Pull steadily on both ends of the marlinspike hitch to capsize the knot. This automatically brings the working end of the line around into a bight and secures the knot.

● The working end has moved across and forms a bight as the knot is tightened. This also give the knot its distinctive trefoil shape at the top.

● This is worth mastering for use with synthetic ropes. However, it is not so easy to tie with your eyes shut as the ordinary bowline.

▶ **over, under, over**   ▶ **tighten**

manharness knot

This is an old and incredibly simple knot that deserves to be widely known. Use it whenever you need a series of loops on a line.

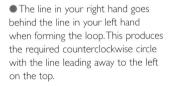

● The traditional use for a manharness knot was to make shoulder loops to haul carts and field-guns. It has also been used to create a series of loops along a picket line for tethering horses during the night.

● The knot is tied in the bight. The first step is to make an counterclockwise overhand loop. This is most easily done by holding the line in both hands and making a half turn.

● The line in your right hand goes behind the line in your left hand when forming the loop. This produces the required counterclockwise circle with the line leading away to the left on the top.

● The next stage is to bring this line down behind the loop, dividing the loop into two equal halves. This is the incomplete overhand knot or marlinspike hitch.

▶   **make an overhand loop**   ▶   **make a marlinspike hitch**

● To finish the knot, pass the right-hand edge of the loop under and then over the center and left-hand parts of the loop.

● Looking at the knot from the front, take the right-hand edge of the loop and pass it under the center line. Then continue to move it left and bring it out over the left-hand edge.

● Hold on to the loop and pull the knot up to tighten it. Make sure that the finished loop is secure and the two hitches are tight enough.

● The finished knot has a distinctive asymmetrical appearance. One of its advantages is that it seldom jams and is easy to undo.

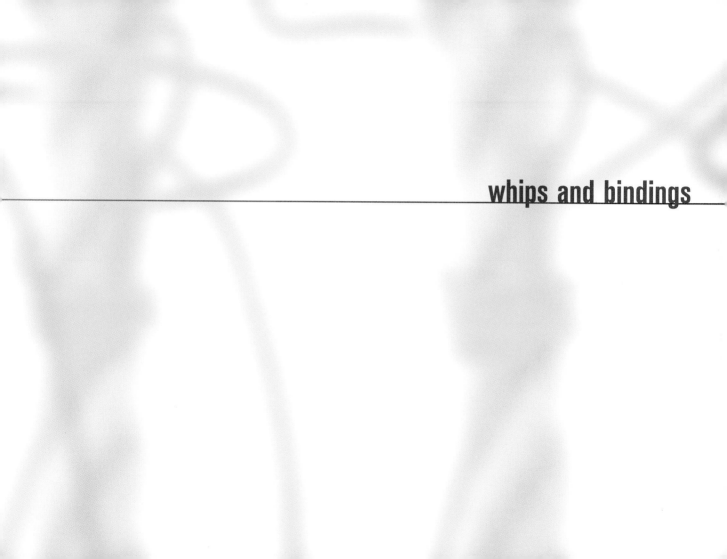

whips and bindings

common whipping

The common whipping is easy to understand and master and is also one of the most secure.

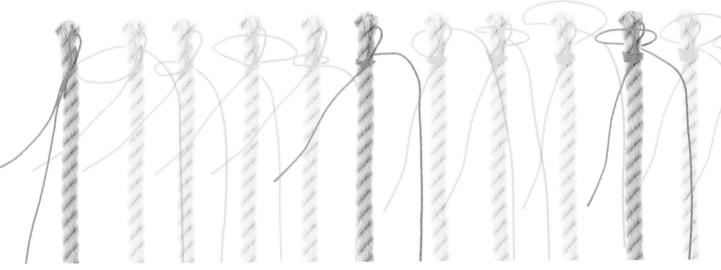

● Whippings were traditionally applied to rope ends to prevent them from fraying and unravelling. They are also useful in a number of other situations, such as splicing two pieces of wood together.

● Today, when ropes are made of synthetic material and the ends can be heat-sealed, whippings are less common. It should be noted that if a rope end is whipped, it should not be heat-sealed in addition.

● The common whipping is easy to apply. Start by making a bight in the whipping cord and place the bight so that it lies at the end of the rope as shown. The whipping should be at least as long as the diameter of the rope.

● Take the working end of the cord and start to wrap it around the rope, working up toward the bight at the end. It is important to trap both parts of the whipping cord under the first turn.

■   ▶ **make a bight**   ▶ **trap the bight with the first turn**

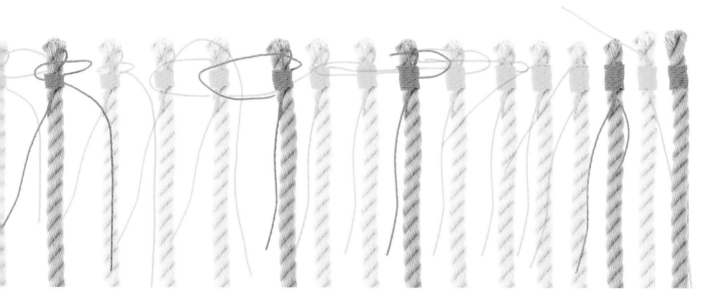

● Continue to lay the turns around the rope, taking care that each turn fits snugly against the preceding one. Pull each turn tight.

● Always work against the lay of the rope so that if the rope starts to unravel, it will only serve to tighten the whipping. Here, the turns are laid down clockwise, from back to front.

● When you have laid down sufficient turns, pass the working end of the whipping cord under the loop at the top of the bight. Pull the last turn tight.

● Pull down on the standing part of the cord trapped underneath the whipping. You may need pliers to help you do this. Pull the bight underneath to the center of the whipping. Trim off both ends neatly.

complete the turns ▶ **pass the end through the bight** ▶ **pull down hard, trim** ■

constrictor knot *and bindings*

Constrictor knots are useful in many situations and can be tied with or without a drawloop.

When tied without a drawloop, they must be cut away carefully. They are particularly useful as semi-permanent seizings on rope's ends.

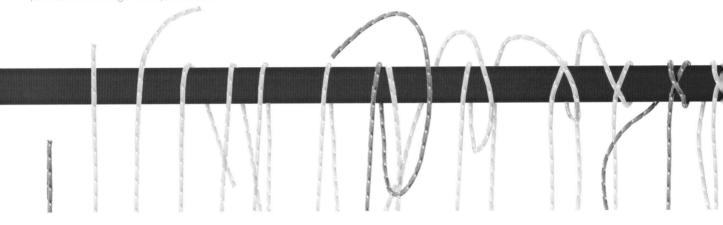

● The constrictor knot is an alternative to the simpler strangle knot, and with some practice, it can be tied extremely quickly, either in the bight or working from one end as shown here.

● It has been suggested that this knot originated in ancient times and was used by the Greeks for surgical slings. It may also have been the "gunner's knot" that secured bags of cartridge gunpowder.

● The constrictor knot can be tied to the left or right. Start by taking a turn around the object that you want to tie from the front to the back.

● Take the turn over and across the standing part of the rope as if you were going to tie a simple clove hitch. The first part of the knot is exactly the same.

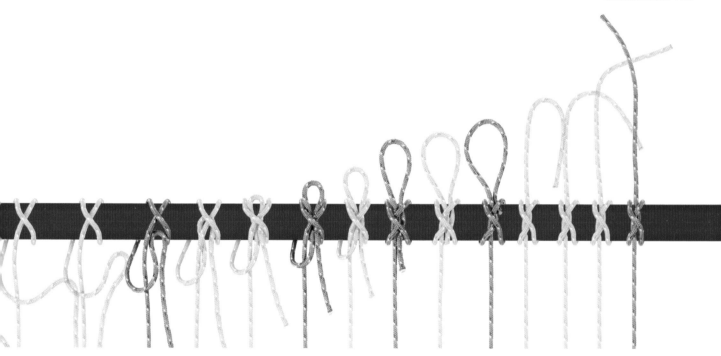

● At this point, the construction of the two knots varies. To complete the clove hitch, the working end of the cord would be passed up under the diagonal to lie parallel with the standing part of the cord.

● When tying the constrictor knot, the working end of the cord is now brought over the standing part and pushed through the center of the diagonal, as shown above.

● You may prefer to do this with a bight of cord, forming a drawloop as shown, for then the knot can be undone. Once it is tied without the drawloop, the overriding diagonal must be cut with a knife to undo it.

● Pull the knot tight, leaving the drawloop in place. If you have tied the knot as a semi-permanent seizing, pull the drawloop through and trim both ends neatly.

▶ **bring a bight through the knot**   ▶ **pull up and tighten**   ■

frustrator knot *whips and bindings*

This is another knot, like the constrictor, that can be used to put a temporary seizing on the end of a rope. Unlike that ancient knot, however, the frustrator was discovered by Dr. Henry Asher in 1986.

● This knot is not quite so easy to tie as the simple strangle knot shown on pages 120–121, but a number of people prefer it. It serves much the same purpose.

● The first step is to take the line over the object you wish to secure, working from the back to the front.

● Loop the working end around the standing part of the line and then take it back up over the point of attachment, this time from the front to the back. Pull the end over to make a twist in the cord.

● Take the uppermost cord over to the left; the frustration knot is completed with the lower cord.

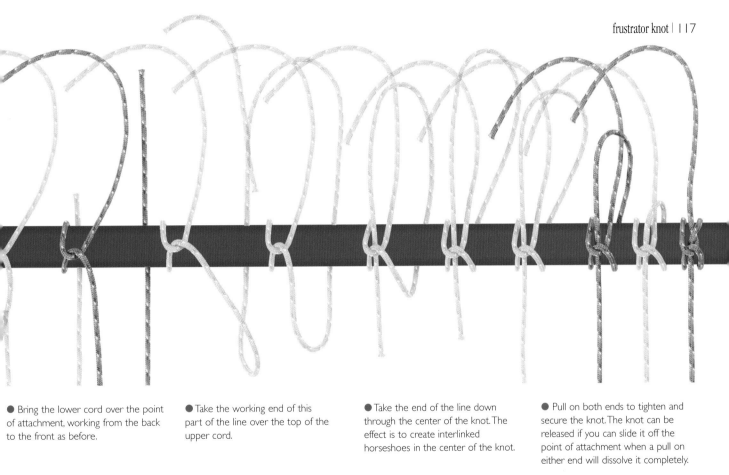

● Bring the lower cord over the point of attachment, working from the back to the front as before.

● Take the working end of this part of the line over the top of the upper cord.

● Take the end of the line down through the center of the knot. The effect is to create interlinked horseshoes in the center of the knot.

● Pull on both ends to tighten and secure the knot. The knot can be released if you can slide it off the point of attachment when a pull on either end will dissolve it completely.

▶ **around behind**　　　　　　　　▶ **down through**　　　　▶ **tighten**

reef knot *and bindings*

The reef, or square, knot is one of the oldest of all knots and was known to the Ancient Egyptians. If it is tied with twin drawloops, it becomes a double bow, the best way to tie shoelaces. However, it is only reliable as a binding knot and should never be used as a bend. Tied with a single drawloop for quick release, it was the knot that was traditionally used to reef sails, hence the name.

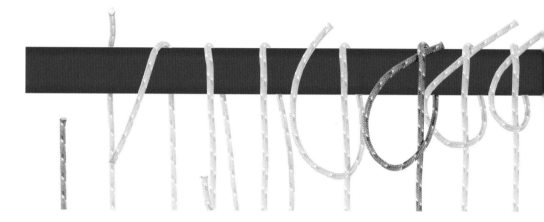

● A mis-tied reef knot—or a granny—can cause problems. Therefore, it is well worth learning how to tie the reef knot correctly.

● The knot is shown here tied around a beam, working with one end of the rope at a time. In practice, it is tied more frequently with both ends at once, for instance matching reef points on either side of a sail.

● Take a turn around the point of attachment and make a single overhand knot. Here, the knot has been made taking the right-hand strand of rope over the left hand.

▶ tie an overhand knot

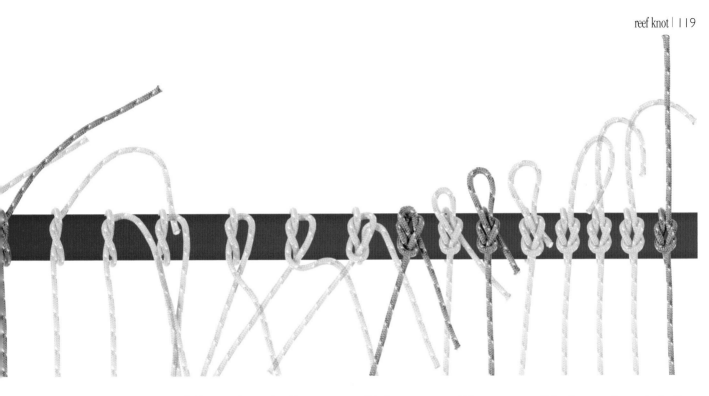

● Bring the top part of the rope, the left-hand strand, down and over the bottom part.

● Make another overhand knot on top of the first. This time, the left-hand rope goes over the right and is pushed through in a drawloop. It can either be left like this or pulled straight.

● It does not matter which way you start tying the knot so long as the second overhand knot is made in the opposite direction; it can be tied either "right over left, left over right," or "left over right, right over left."

● Another way of remembering the correct way is to lay the working ends and standing parts of the line next to each other when you make the second overhand knot.

▶ **and back the other way**　　　　　▶ **tighten**

strangle knot *whips and bindings*

The strangle knot is probably the simplest of all the binding knots and just as effective as any. It can be used in place of the constrictor knot (see pages 114–115) to seize cut ends of cordage or to hold together objects while they are being glued.

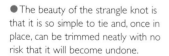

● The beauty of the strangle knot is that it is so simple to tie and, once in place, can be trimmed neatly with no risk that it will become undone.

● It is a very practical way of securing rolls of carpet when used with a fairly substantial cord. The same knot can be employed to keep rolls of paper in place.

● The knot is a simple double overhand knot that is here shown tied around a beam. It can also be tied on its own and left loose. The object to be secured can then be slipped into the knot before it is tightened.

● Take the first turn around the point of attachment, working from the front to the back as shown above.

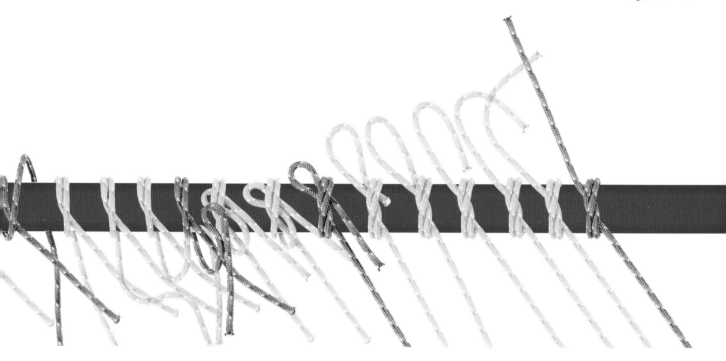

● Take a second turn alongside the first. Both turns cross the standing part of the line.

● Complete the knot by passing the working end under both of the turns, forming a double overhand knot. Here the end is being pushed under the turns on the bight. This enables the knot to be released easily.

● If you want, you can pull the knot tight at this stage, although it is not quite as secure at the completed knot.

● The bight has been pulled through. Tighten both ends to make the knot totally secure. When you check the knot, make sure that the overriding diagonal lies between the other two parts of the knot. Trim the ends.

▶ **and another**   ▶ **go under both turns**   ▶ **pull through and tighten** ■

double figure-of-eight binding

The double figure-of-eight binding has little in common with the figure-of-eight knot and the result is similar to a double clove hitch. It is sometimes called the double figure-of-eight hitch.

● The figure-of-eight binding is tied in the bight and kept open. The end of the rope, or other object that you want to secure, is then inserted into the knot before it is tightened.

● Start making the figure-of-eight by making a clockwise loop on the left. The working end is at the front of the loop.

● Bring the line across and make an opposite loop on the right. The working end now lies on top of the loop as shown.

● Make another loop with the same end, this time on the left, laying the loop on top of the first loop. The line remains on the top of the coil, leading back to the right and pointing downward.

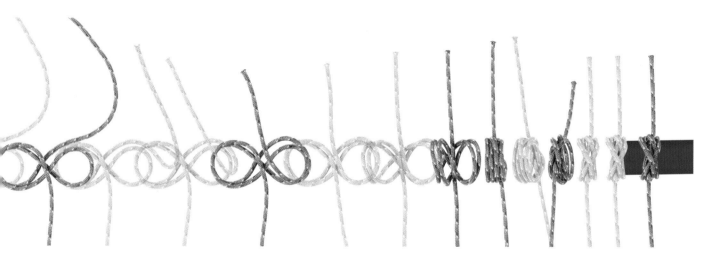

● Complete the last figure-of-eight with the other end of the line, which was used to form the first loop. Make this loop on top of the right-hand loop with the end of the line on the top of the two figures of eight.

● The initial part of the knot is now complete. Note that both working parts of the line are in the center of the figures-of-eight.

● Pick up all the loops and fold them inward so the working parts of the line remain in the center of the binding.

● Slip the binding over a spar or the end of a rope and gradually tighten the binding by pulling on both ends until the knot is totally secure. Trim the ends neatly to finish.

bracelet binding

whips and bindings

This is a simple, yet attractive, knot with a neat appearance. Care must be taken, when tightening, to make the most of its ornamental form.

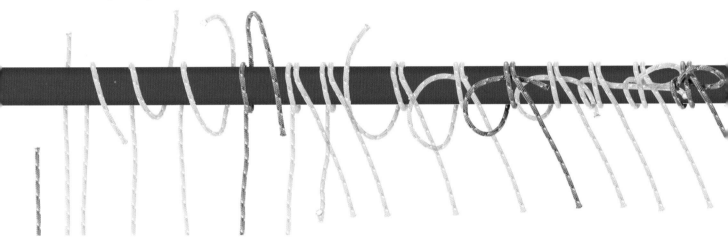

● This binding is more decorative than the others. It is quite simple in theory, but more difficult to tie correctly in practice. It is also difficult to tighten.

● Start by taking your line behind the point of attachment and make a complete turn over the bar. Both ends of the line should hang down, the one on the right at the front and the other on the left at the rear.

● Pick up the left-hand line, bring it around to the front, and feed it behind the two loops on the bar as shown.

● Pull the line through, leaving a bight. Then, take the working end back through the bight, tying a half hitch around itself. It is important that this hitch is made from front to back.

● This hitch is the top one of the two that complete the knot. To make the second hitch, take the other end of the line and pass it underneath the two strands at the bottom of the first hitch.

● This forms a bight. To complete the binding take the end of the line back through this bight.

● Take the line through the bight, again taking it through from the front to the back. Pull on both ends to tighten the knot.

● This makes a secure quatrefoil (four-crowned) symmetrical knot that can serve as a bracelet. It is difficult to tighten around the end of a rope or spar.

make a second hitch ▶ **take line through bight** ▶

index